The Heart of Partners Redefining Love, Inti Commitment

Azhar ul Haque Sario

Copyright

Contents

Part 1: Deconstructing the Modern Relationship Landscape

The Evolving Tapestry of Gender Dynamics

Beyond "Boy Meets Girl": Love, Fluidity, and the Evolving Heart of Relationships

Forget the dusty rulebook of "boy meets girl." Love in the 21st century is a vibrant, ever-shifting landscape, painted in hues far beyond the traditional pink and blue. We're finally waking up to the beautiful truth: gender isn't a static point on a line, but a spectrum, a dance, a story that unfolds over time. This realization is revolutionizing how we connect, how we love, and how we build our lives together.

For generations, we've been handed a pre-packaged narrative of relationships. Man plays provider, woman nurtures. He's strong and silent, she's emotional and supportive. But these roles, like ill-fitting costumes, often chafe and restrict. They ignore the infinite variations of human experience, the messy, beautiful reality that we are all unique individuals, regardless of our assigned sex at birth.

Think of gender as a verb, not a noun. It's something we do, something we express, something that evolves within us. We're seeing a blossoming of language to reflect this: genderqueer, non-binary, genderfluid, agender – each term a brushstroke in the ever-expanding portrait of identity. These aren't just labels; they're windows into the lived experiences of people who have bravely stepped outside the confines of the binary.

And what happens when these individuals fall in love? That's where things get truly interesting. Traditional relationship models, built on the foundation of rigid gender roles, simply don't fit anymore. We're seeing a beautiful explosion of diversity in relationships: same-sex couples, polyamorous arrangements, partnerships that defy categorization altogether. Love, in its infinite wisdom, is finding new forms.

Imagine a couple where one partner realizes they're genderfluid. This isn't just a personal revelation; it's a shared journey. Suddenly, the comfortable map of their relationship is redrawn. Communication becomes paramount. They have to talk – really talk – about their feelings, their fears, their hopes. They have to learn a new language of intimacy, one that honors the fluidity of identity.

Maybe the division of labor shifts. Perhaps the partner who once identified as male finds joy in traditionally "feminine" tasks, or vice versa. Maybe their sexual dynamic evolves, requiring a renegotiation of boundaries and desires. It's a process of discovery, of shedding old assumptions and embracing the unknown.

These shifts aren't always easy. There can be societal pressures, family misunderstandings, even internal struggles. But couples who navigate these challenges with open hearts and a willingness to learn often find themselves with a deeper, more authentic connection. They've built their love on a foundation of truth, not pre-conceived notions.

We need more research to understand the nuances of these relationships. But what we already know is this: acceptance is key. When partners feel seen, understood, and celebrated for who they are, their love flourishes. When they're forced to conform, it withers.

So, let's throw out the old rulebook. Let's celebrate the beautiful chaos of love in all its forms. Let's embrace the fluidity of gender and the infinite possibilities of human connection. The future of love isn't about fitting into boxes; it's about creating our own. It's about two hearts, or three, or more, finding a rhythm that works for them, a dance that's uniquely their own. And that, my friends, is something truly beautiful.

The Dance of Equals: Rethinking Power in Modern Love

Remember when relationships were like a rigid waltz, one partner leading, the other following? These days, love looks more like a dynamic tango, a constant negotiation of steps, where sometimes you lead, sometimes you lean, and sometimes you just hold each other close. The landscape of modern romance has dramatically shifted, and nowhere is that change more apparent than in the evolving dance of power.

We've moved away from the era where men automatically held the reins, their authority often rooted in economic control and societal expectations. Women, often relegated to the domestic sphere, frequently had limited access to resources and decision-making power.

But the world has changed. Women's increased access to education and economic independence has rewritten the rules, and evolving attitudes toward gender roles have blurred the lines of traditional masculinity and femininity.

This isn't just about societal shifts; it's about a fundamental human desire for connection based on mutual respect and genuine partnership. Think of it like this: have you ever tried to build a sandcastle with one person dictating every detail? It's frustrating! Real magic happens when everyone gets to contribute their unique vision, their individual "sand." That's the essence of an egalitarian relationship.

What does this new dance look like?

It's about shared decisions, not dictated ones. It's about valuing each other's opinions, even when they differ. It's about open communication, the kind where you can be vulnerable and know you'll be met with understanding, not judgment. It's about dividing the "chores of life" – from laundry to childcare – in a way that feels fair, acknowledging that "fair" isn't always a perfect 50/50 split, but rather a fluid agreement that adapts to life's ever-changing rhythm.

The Myth of Perfect Equality:

Let's be real: "perfect" equality is a myth, like finding a unicorn riding a bicycle. Subtle power dynamics will always exist. Maybe one partner has a higher income, or perhaps one is more emotionally expressive. These "power currencies," as we might call them, can influence the relationship. The key isn't to eradicate all power differences (which is probably impossible), but to be aware of them and navigate them consciously.

The Bumps in the Road:

Navigating these new dynamics isn't always smooth sailing. Internalized gender roles can sneak in like unwelcome guests, influencing our behavior even when we consciously reject them. Societal pressures can feel like a nagging backseat driver, urging you to conform to old-fashioned relationship models. And let's not forget the daily grind of balancing work, family, and personal needs. It's a lot!

Consider this: Sarah and David, both ambitious lawyers, decided early on to share everything – from household chores to childcare – equally. They even have a shared online calendar color-coded for each family member. But recently, Sarah's career took off, requiring longer hours and more travel. David, while supportive, started to feel the weight of the increased domestic load. This wasn't about one person being "right" or "wrong"; it was about the ever-shifting balance of their lives and the need to renegotiate their "dance."

The Power of Conflict:

Conflict is often seen as a relationship killer, but in egalitarian relationships, it can actually be a catalyst for growth. When handled constructively, disagreements can illuminate hidden power dynamics and create opportunities for deeper understanding. It's about learning to communicate effectively, to listen without defensiveness, and to find solutions that work for both partners.

The Rewards of Equality:

Why bother with all this, you might ask? Well, the rewards are significant. Egalitarian relationships are linked to higher relationship satisfaction, improved well-being for both partners, stronger parent-child bonds, and even greater sexual satisfaction. When both partners feel valued, respected, and heard, the connection deepens, creating a love that is both passionate and enduring.

The Future of Love:

As society continues to evolve, so too will our understanding of love and partnership. The dance of equals is not just a trend; it's a reflection of our growing desire for authentic connection, mutual respect, and shared power. It's about creating relationships where both partners can thrive, individually and together. And that, I think, is a dance worth learning.

The Myth of "Having It All": More Like Juggling Flaming Torches While Riding a Unicycle

Let's be honest, the phrase "having it all" feels less like a celebratory achievement and more like a pressure cooker about to burst. It paints a picture of a woman gliding effortlessly through life, career soaring, family adoring, personal life flourishing. Spoiler alert: that picture is a fantasy. The reality, for many women, is a chaotic symphony of competing demands, often leaving them feeling more like they're juggling flaming torches while riding a unicycle than gracefully "having it all."

From Domestic Goddess to Superwoman: A History of Shifting Expectations (and Zero Extra Hours in the Day)

Think back a few decades. Women were largely expected to find fulfillment in the home. Marriage and motherhood were the ultimate goals. Fast forward to today, and while we've made incredible strides in shattering glass ceilings and entering the workforce, the old expectations haven't exactly vanished. Instead, they've multiplied. Now, women are expected to not only excel in their careers but also be super-moms, Pinterest-perfect homemakers, and endlessly supportive partners. It's like we've traded in one set of expectations for a far more demanding one, without being given a time-turner to manage it all.

The Career-Relationship Conundrum: A False Choice

One of the biggest lies we've been told is that career ambition and fulfilling relationships are mutually exclusive. It's a narrative that pits two essential parts of life against each other, forcing women to feel like they have to choose. This is often fueled by societal expectations and those pesky gender stereotypes that whisper in our ears. Think about it: how often do you hear a man being asked how he balances his career and family? Exactly.

The truth is, demanding careers often require long hours and travel, making it difficult to nurture relationships. On the flip side, prioritizing family can sometimes lead to career plateaus, leaving women feeling unfulfilled. It's a tightrope walk with no safety net.

The Weight of the World (and the Dishes): Societal Expectations and the Second Shift

Let's talk about the invisible load. Women are often socialized from a young age to prioritize marriage and motherhood, while men are pushed towards career success. This ingrained messaging can create a constant internal tug-of-war. And even when both partners work full-time, women often shoulder the lion's share of domestic duties – the infamous "second shift." Research backs this up: women still spend significantly more time on housework and childcare. It's exhausting, and it's a major contributor to the feeling of being overwhelmed.

The Workplace Maze: Bias, Burnout, and the "Boys' Club"

Even in workplaces with seemingly progressive policies, women often face subtle (and sometimes not-so-subtle) discrimination. Implicit bias, lack of mentorship, and the lingering "boys' club" mentality can make climbing the corporate ladder feel like an uphill battle. And let's not forget the "mommy tax" – the often-unspoken penalty women face for taking time off to care for children.

The Ripple Effect: Relationships Under Pressure

All of this takes a toll. The constant juggling act can lead to stress, exhaustion, and resentment, straining relationships with partners, kids, and even friends. The division of labor at home can become a major point of contention, especially when one partner feels like they're carrying more than their fair share.

Real Women, Real Struggles: Case Studies in the Chaos

The Tech Executive: She's at the top of her game, but her biological clock is ticking. The pressure to "lean in" at work clashes with her desire to start a family. She feels like she's being pulled in two directions, constantly questioning her choices.

The Working Mom: She's found a balance with part-time work, but her career has stalled. She feels overlooked for promotions and struggles with the feeling that she's not reaching her full potential.

The Entrepreneur: She's built her dream business from the ground up, but her personal life is suffering. The demands of running a company leave little time for her relationship, and she's starting to feel isolated.

Redefining "Having It All": It's About My All, Not Their All

The traditional definition of "having it all" is a myth, a trap, a recipe for burnout. It's time to redefine what success looks like, not based on societal expectations, but on our own individual values.

Smash the Stereotypes: We need to challenge the ingrained gender stereotypes that hold women back. This means calling out bias, demanding equal pay, and pushing for policies that support working families.

Equality Isn't Optional: True gender equality requires dismantling the systemic barriers that prevent women from reaching their full potential.

Flexibility, Not Just Lip Service: Companies need to walk the walk when it comes to flexible work arrangements. It's not just about offering options, it's about creating a culture where women feel supported, not penalized, for using them.

Communication is Key: Open and honest communication within families is crucial. Partners need to work together to create a division of labor that feels fair and sustainable.

Self-Care is Not Selfish: Women need to prioritize their own well-being. This means setting boundaries, saying "no," and making time for themselves.

Rewrite the Rules of Success: Success isn't a one-size-fits-all concept. It's about defining what matters most to you and creating a life that reflects those values.

Ultimately, "having it all" isn't about achieving some impossible ideal. It's about making conscious choices, prioritizing what truly matters, and creating a life that feels authentic and fulfilling – on your terms. It's about building your all, not someone else's.

The Man in the Mirror: Rethinking Masculinity in the 21st Century

Let's talk about men. For generations, the image of the "real man" has been carved from granite: stoic, strong, the provider, the protector. Emotions? Best kept locked away in a vault. Vulnerability? A sign of weakness. This "man box," as it's often called, might have served a purpose in another era, but in today's world, it's doing more harm than good. It's time for a serious conversation about what it truly means to be a man in the 21st century.

Imagine a man carrying a heavy burden. He's told to smile, to shoulder it all without complaint. Inside, he might be crumbling, but the world expects him to be the rock. This isn't strength; it's a recipe for disaster. We're seeing the consequences: higher rates of suicide, addiction, and anger issues among men. It's not that men don't feel; it's that they've been told they shouldn't.

Think back. Our grandfathers, maybe even our fathers, grew up in a world where men were defined by their physical prowess and their ability to provide. Emotions were for women. This wasn't malicious; it was just the way things were. But the world has changed. The feminist movement, the fight for LGBTQ+ rights, and a growing awareness of mental health have challenged these outdated norms. We're finally starting to realize that this "man box" is suffocating everyone, men included.

Now, men find themselves in a tricky spot. Society tells them to be strong, but also sensitive. Assertive, but compassionate. Successful, but emotionally available. It's a confusing tightrope walk, and many men are understandably unsure where to put their feet. They're caught between the old ideals and the new expectations, unsure how to define their masculinity in a way that feels authentic.

One of the biggest hurdles is the stigma around mental health. Even though we've made progress, many men still hesitate to seek help. That old idea of vulnerability as weakness lingers. They fear judgment, ridicule. But here's the truth: vulnerability isn't weakness; it's courage. It takes real strength to look inward, to acknowledge your struggles, and to ask for help.

Think about it. Isn't it more powerful to face your emotions than to bury them? Vulnerability allows men to connect with others on a deeper level, to build stronger relationships. It's how we heal from trauma and develop resilience. It's not about becoming a different person; it's about becoming a whole person.

And what about emotional expression? Men need to feel safe to express the full range of human emotions, not just anger. Sadness, fear, joy – they're all part of the human experience. Learning to identify and articulate these emotions is key to building healthy relationships and managing stress. It's about developing emotional literacy, and it's a skill that can be learned.

We're seeing positive changes. Men's support groups are popping up everywhere, both online and in person. They offer a safe space for men to connect, share their experiences, and challenge these old ideas about masculinity. The #MeToo movement, while focused on sexual harassment, has also sparked a much-needed conversation about toxic masculinity. And when celebrities and athletes open up about their own mental health struggles, they help to normalize the conversation and show other men that they're not alone.

This isn't just a "men's issue"; it's a human issue. Redefining masculinity is about creating a world where everyone, regardless of gender, can thrive. It's about giving men permission to be themselves, to embrace their full humanity, and to redefine what it means to be a man in the 21st century. It's a work in progress, but it's a journey worth taking. The man in the mirror deserves nothing less.

The Algorithmic Heart: Technology and the Future of Dating

Love in the Time of Algorithms: A Heart in the Machine

The digital revolution hasn't just changed how we order pizza; it's rewritten the entire playbook of love. Online dating, once the domain of the tech-savvy and romantically challenged, has become the de facto town square for modern courtship. We swipe right, we match, we chat, all mediated by the invisible hand of the algorithm. But what happens to our hearts, our hopes, and our heads in this brave new world of digital romance?

Swiping Through Souls (or Something Like It): The User Experience

Imagine a bustling marketplace, but instead of fruits and vegetables, you're browsing faces and curated snippets of personality. That's the modern dating app. We enter this digital arena with a kaleidoscope of motivations. Some seek a fleeting spark, a connection as ephemeral as a Snapchat story. Others yearn for a soulmate, a love story worthy of a Hollywood rom-com. Age, gender, location – these factors paint the broad strokes of our desires. But beneath the surface lies a complex tapestry of personalities and attachment styles.

The securely attached dater approaches the app with a balanced perspective, seeking genuine connection without losing themselves in the digital vortex. They're the pragmatists of the online world. Then there are the anxiously attached, forever refreshing their notifications, each ping a potential validation (or crushing disappointment). And finally, the avoidant daters, dipping their toes in the pool of romance but recoiling at the first sign of vulnerability, leaving a trail of unanswered messages in their wake.

The apps themselves are masterful puppeteers of our behavior. The swipe, the match, the dopamine hit – it's a gamified experience designed to keep us hooked. We become connoisseurs of curated selfies and witty bios, judging potential partners in the blink of an eye. But this constant stream of choices can also lead to a strange paradox: an abundance of options can lead to a sense of emptiness, a fear that the perfect match is always just one swipe away, leaving us perpetually searching but never truly satisfied.

The Algorithm: Cupid's Coded Wingman (or Not)

At the heart of this digital dance of love lies the algorithm, a mysterious formula whispered to be the key to romantic bliss. These digital matchmakers consider everything from our star signs (just kidding... mostly) to our favorite pizza toppings. Some algorithms are as simple as a high school compatibility quiz, while others delve into the depths of personality assessments, attempting to predict long-term relationship success.

But can an algorithm truly understand the messy, irrational, and beautiful chaos of human connection? Can it quantify the spark that ignites between two souls? While these algorithms can efficiently filter through a sea of potential partners, they often struggle to capture the nuances of human compatibility. Emotional intelligence, communication styles, shared values – these are the ingredients of lasting love, and they're not easily reducible to data points.

And let's not forget the biases lurking within the code. Algorithms are trained on data, and if that data reflects societal prejudices, the algorithm will perpetuate them. This can lead to discriminatory outcomes, reinforcing existing inequalities in the dating world. The "black box" nature of these algorithms only adds to the mystery and the potential for unfairness. We're entrusting our love lives to a system we don't fully understand.

The Heart's GPS: Navigating the Emotional Terrain

Dating apps have undeniably democratized the search for love, connecting people across geographical boundaries and social circles. But they've also ushered in a new set of emotional challenges. The constant judgment, the ghosting, the curated perfection – it can take a toll on our self-esteem. A rejected match can feel like a personal slight, and the pressure to present a flawless online persona can fuel anxiety and insecurity.

The sheer volume of choices can also lead to "choice overload," leaving us paralyzed by possibilities. We become trapped in a cycle of swiping, never truly investing in a connection for fear that something better is just around the corner. And the ease of online interaction can sometimes come at the expense of genuine empathy and communication skills. It's easier to ghost someone with a tap than to have an honest conversation about why things aren't working.

But amidst the digital noise, there are stories of love blossoming from a right swipe. For those who struggle to meet people in their daily lives, dating apps can be a lifeline, a way to connect with like-minded individuals and find community. They can be especially valuable for marginalized groups who may find it easier to connect with others who share their experiences.

The Future of Digital Love: A More Human Approach

As we navigate this new era of digital romance, we need to be mindful of the psychological impact of these platforms. Researchers are exploring ways to mitigate the negative effects of social comparison and choice overload, while developers are working on algorithms that prioritize genuine compatibility over superficial metrics.

Perhaps the future of online dating lies in a more human-centered approach. Imagine apps that encourage meaningful conversations, that foster empathy and respect, that prioritize emotional intelligence over curated selfies. Imagine algorithms that not only match us based on shared interests but also help us develop the communication skills needed for lasting relationships.

Ultimately, the key is to remember that technology is just a tool. It can connect us, but it can't replace the messy, vulnerable, and ultimately human experience of falling in love. The heart still beats in the age of algorithms, and it's up to us to use these tools wisely, to cultivate genuine connection, and to remember that love, in all its complexity, is still the most human of pursuits.

2.2: Digital Intimacy: More Than Just Emojis and Memes

Let's be real, the digital world has completely flipped the script on intimacy. Remember when "quality time" meant actually being with someone? Now, it can mean tagging them in a meme or reacting to their Instagram story. It's not necessarily bad, just...different. This isn't your grandma's idea of romance, that's for sure.

So, what is digital intimacy anyway? It's that feeling of connection, vulnerability, and understanding, but woven through the fabric of our online lives. It's how we build and maintain relationships in a world that's increasingly digital-first. Think about it: how many relationships started with a DM slide? How many are kept alive by late-night texts? This is our reality.

From Handwritten Letters to Heart Emojis:

Intimacy used to be about whispered secrets and shared glances. Now, it's about carefully curated Instagram posts and perfectly timed GIFs. Technology has given us superpowers of connection. We can chat with someone across the globe as easily as we can talk to the person next door. This hyper-connectivity has its perks. Loneliness can feel less crushing when you have a community of online friends. Long-distance relationships can thrive with constant video calls. It's like having a pocketful of potential connections.

But, like any superpower, it comes with a few kryptonite-sized challenges.

The Double-Edged Sword of Digital Connection:

Asynchronous Communication: The Art of the Delayed Reply: While crafting the perfect text can be a blessing, it can also be a curse. Think about how much anxiety a "seen" message can cause. We overthink, we analyze, we catastrophize. It's a breeding ground for misinterpretations and hurt feelings. Where's the spontaneity gone?

Visual and Auditory Communication: Beyond the Selfie: Video calls and voice notes are the closest we get to real-life interaction online. They add a layer of humanity to digital communication. But even then, it's a curated version of ourselves. We're all guilty of angling the camera just right, right?

Self-Disclosure and Vulnerability: Sharing Your Soul (with a Filter): Online platforms can feel like a safe space to share. Anonymity can be liberating. But remember, the internet is forever. That vulnerable post you shared might come back to haunt you. There's a fine line between sharing and oversharing.

Social Media: The Relationship Rollercoaster:

Social media is the ultimate relationship playground – and battleground.

Relationship Initiation: Swiping Right for Romance: Dating apps have revolutionized matchmaking. But let's be honest, it's a highlight reel, not the real deal. We're judging people based on a few photos and a witty bio. Where's the awkward first date jitters?

Relationship Maintenance: Keeping the Spark Alive (Online): Sharing memes and tagging your partner in posts is the modern equivalent of sending flowers. But constant online interaction can also lead to obsessive checking and social media-fueled jealousy.

Self-Presentation and Identity: The Curated Self: We're all guilty of presenting the best version of ourselves online. It's a performance. But what happens when the online persona clashes with reality?

Conflict and Jealousy: The Green-Eyed Monster Goes Digital: Social media is a breeding ground for jealousy. Seeing your partner interact with others can trigger insecurities. It's so easy to misinterpret a comment or read too much into a like.

The Dark Side of Digital Intimacy:

Misinterpretation and Miscommunication: Lost in Translation: Without body language and tone of voice, it's easy to misinterpret digital communication. Sarcasm can be lost, jokes can fall flat, and misunderstandings can spiral out of control.

Privacy and Security: The Price of Sharing: Sharing personal information online is risky. Data breaches and hacking are real threats. We need to be more aware of what we share and who we share it with.

Addiction and Excessive Use: Lost in the Scroll: It's easy to get sucked into the digital vortex. Scrolling for hours can lead to neglecting real-life relationships and create feelings of isolation.

Superficial Connections: A Mile Wide, an Inch Deep: We can have thousands of online friends but still feel incredibly lonely. It's important to prioritize quality over quantity when it comes to relationships.

The Future of Digital Intimacy: Beyond the Screen:

VR and AR are poised to take digital intimacy to the next level. Imagine sharing a virtual sunset with your partner, even if you're miles apart. The possibilities are endless.

But as we embrace these new technologies, we need to be mindful of the potential pitfalls. We need to cultivate digital literacy, prioritize real-life connections, and remember that technology is a tool, not a replacement for human interaction.

Digital intimacy is a complex and evolving landscape. It's a reflection of our times, a mix of connection and isolation, vulnerability and curated perfection. Navigating this world requires awareness, intention, and a healthy dose of skepticism. It's about finding a balance between the digital and the real, and remembering that true intimacy is about genuine human connection, whether it's through a screen or across a table.

The Hookup Culture: A Rollercoaster of Liberation and Heartache

Let's talk about hookup culture. It's the elephant in the room (or maybe the Tinder profile on your phone) for many young adults today. It's this swirling mix of freedom, fun, and sometimes, a hefty dose of "what just happened?"

Imagine a world where "Netflix and chill" has become a globally understood euphemism, where relationship statuses are as fluid as the latest TikTok trend, and where the lines between "just sex" and "something more" are blurrier than a late-night selfie. That's hookup culture in a nutshell. It's the soundtrack of a generation exploring intimacy in a world that's both hyper-connected and strangely isolating.

But let's be real, it's not all sunshine and fleeting make-out sessions. This landscape of casual encounters can be as exhilarating as it is emotionally treacherous. It's a complex beast, and we need to unpack it.

Hooking Up: What's the Deal?

First, let's define our terms. "Hooking up" can mean anything from a drunken kiss at a party to a more intimate encounter, often without the expectation of a committed relationship. It's the "let's see where this goes...or maybe not" approach to dating. Think of it as the appetizer before the main course of committed relationships, or for some, perhaps the entire meal.

This phenomenon is particularly prevalent on college campuses, where the freedom of being away from home and the pressure to "experience" everything can be intense. But it's not just a college thing. Young professionals are also navigating this terrain, trying to balance career goals with their personal lives, often finding that the simplicity of a hookup fits their current lifestyle.

Several factors have contributed to the rise of hookup culture. Birth control has given people more control over their reproductive choices, separating sex from the risk of pregnancy. Dating apps have made finding a potential partner as easy as ordering a pizza (and sometimes just as satisfying, or not). And let's not forget the influence of media, which often portrays casual sex as glamorous and consequence-free.

The Emotional Minefield

Now, here's where things get interesting, and often, a little messy. Hookup culture can be incredibly liberating for some. They feel empowered, sexually autonomous, and free from the constraints of traditional relationship expectations. It's a chance to explore their sexuality without the pressure of commitment.

But for others, it can be an emotional rollercoaster. The lack of clear communication and expectations can lead to hurt feelings, confusion, and even regret. Imagine waking up after a hookup feeling more empty than fulfilled. Or developing feelings for someone who only sees you as a casual fling. These experiences can be emotionally bruising.

Research has shown that women, in particular, may be more vulnerable to negative emotional consequences after a hookup. This could be due to societal pressures and the double standard that often exists around female sexuality. It's also possible that women, on average, place a greater emphasis on emotional connection within sexual encounters.

Real People, Real Stories (Hypothetical, of Course)

Let's imagine a few scenarios:

Sarah: A bright and ambitious college student, jumps into hookup culture with both feet. She enjoys the initial thrill and the feeling of independence. But after a while, she starts to feel a nagging sense of loneliness. She realizes that she craves more than just physical intimacy; she wants emotional connection.

David: A young professional, finds hookups to be the perfect solution for his busy life. He doesn't have time for a serious relationship, but he still desires physical intimacy. He's comfortable with the casual nature of these encounters and feels no pressure to take things further.

Maria: After a hookup with someone she thought she was developing a connection with, Maria is left feeling hurt and confused. The guy made it clear he wasn't looking for anything serious, leaving Maria feeling used and emotionally exposed. She realizes that hookup culture isn't for her.

Navigating the Landscape

So, where do we go from here? There's no easy answer. Hookup culture is a reality, and we need to talk about it openly and honestly. We need to acknowledge the potential benefits and the potential harms.

Education is key. Young adults need to be equipped with the tools to navigate this landscape safely and responsibly. This includes understanding consent, communication, and the importance of respecting boundaries. We also need to promote emotional literacy and provide resources for those who are struggling with the emotional fallout of casual encounters.

And let's not forget about the double standard. We need to challenge the gendered judgments that often surround hookup culture. Women should not be shamed for exploring their sexuality, just as men shouldn't be pressured to be "players."

Hookup culture is a complex and ever-evolving phenomenon. It's a reflection of our changing attitudes towards sex, relationships, and intimacy. By fostering open communication, promoting emotional well-being, and challenging outdated gender norms, we can create a healthier and more supportive environment for young adults as they navigate this brave new world of connection.

Navigating the Minefield of Love: A Guide to Online Dating Safety

Online dating: it's the modern-day equivalent of bumping into someone cute at the library, only now the library is the entire internet and the cute someone could be... well, anyone. While the promise of finding "the one" with a few swipes is undeniably alluring, it's also vital to remember that the digital world isn't always what it seems. Think of it like exploring a new city – exciting, but you wouldn't wander down every dark alley, right? This guide is your map to navigating the sometimes treacherous terrain of online romance, helping you find connection without falling victim to scams, catfishing, or harassment.

The Sweet Talk and the Sting: Recognizing Online Scams

Let's face it, we've all heard stories of someone's grandma's friend who lost their life savings to a charming "doctor" stationed overseas. These scams aren't just urban legends; they're a real threat. Scammers are masters of manipulation, preying on emotions and exploiting vulnerabilities. They build trust, weave elaborate tales, and then, when they've got you hooked, they strike.

Think of it this way: if someone you've never met is professing their undying love within a week and simultaneously asking for a "small loan" to help them get back home, it's a giant red flag waving in your face. No matter how convincing their story, never send money to someone you haven't met in person. It's like giving a stranger on the street your credit card – a recipe for disaster.

Common Scam Tactics: A Rogues' Gallery

The Romeo/Juliet Ploy: Instant soulmates, whirlwind romances, and declarations of eternal love – all within the first few days. Slow down! Genuine connections take time.

The Damsel (or Dude) in Distress: Sudden emergencies, medical bills, car troubles, you name it. There's always a sob story and a desperate plea for cash.

The Investment Guru: "Guaranteed" returns, exclusive opportunities, and pressure to act fast. If it sounds too good to be true, it probably is.

The Gift Card Gambit: Requests for gift cards are a classic scammer move. These are basically untraceable cash, and once you send them, they're gone.

Case Study: The Tinder Swindler – A Cautionary Tale

Remember the Netflix documentary? It's a chilling reminder of how easily charm and charisma can mask malicious intent. This guy wasn't just after money; he was after emotional control, leaving a trail of broken hearts and empty bank accounts. It's a stark reminder that even the most savvy among us can be fooled.

Prevention Strategies: Your Armor Against the Heartless

Verify, Verify, Verify: Reverse image search is your best friend. A quick Google search can reveal if those stunning photos are actually stock images or belong to someone else entirely.

Trust Your Gut: If something feels off, it probably is. Don't ignore those nagging doubts.

Talk to Someone: Share your experiences with a trusted friend or family member. They can offer an objective perspective and help you spot red flags you might have missed.

Catfishing: When the Photo Doesn't Match the Person

Catfishing is like showing up to a date expecting Ryan Gosling and finding... well, not Ryan Gosling. It's the art of creating a fake online persona, often using stolen photos and fabricated information. Sometimes it's driven by insecurity, sometimes by something far more sinister.

Identifying a Catfish: Signs of Deception

Ghosting 101: They avoid video calls like the plague and always have a convenient excuse for why they can't meet in person.

The Vanishing Act: Their social media presence is practically non-existent, or their profiles are brand new with very little activity.

Inconsistent Stories: Their details keep changing, and their stories don't quite add up.

Prevention Strategies: Don't Get Hooked

Demand a Video Chat: It's the easiest way to confirm someone's identity. If they refuse, it's a major red flag.

Do Your Research: Check their social media profiles. Do they have friends? Do their photos look genuine?

Listen to Your Instincts: If something feels fishy, trust your gut.

Online Harassment: Drawing the Line

Online dating should be fun, not frightening. Harassment, from unwanted explicit messages to cyberstalking, is never okay.

Types of Harassment: From Annoying to Alarming

Creepy Comments: Unsolicited sexual remarks, inappropriate jokes, and persistent unwanted messages.

Cyberstalking: Relentless messaging, following your online activity, and making you feel unsafe.

Doxing: Sharing your personal information online without your consent.

Prevention Strategies: Taking Control

Privacy is Power: Adjust your privacy settings on dating apps and social media to limit who can see your profile and contact you.

Block and Report: Don't hesitate to block and report anyone who's making you uncomfortable.

Document Everything: Keep screenshots of harassing messages. This evidence can be helpful if you need to report the abuse to the platform or law enforcement.

Staying Safe in the Digital Dating World: A Final Word

Online dating can be a fantastic way to meet new people, but it's crucial to be aware of the risks. By following these tips and trusting your instincts, you can navigate the world of online romance safely and confidently. Remember, your safety and well-being are paramount. Don't be afraid to take a step back, reassess a situation, and protect yourself. Happy dating!

The Language of Love: Emotional Intelligence and Relationship Success

Decoding the Emotional Symphony: A Journey into Emotional Literacy

Ever feel like your emotions are a runaway train, careening through your inner landscape with no conductor in sight? Or maybe you're trying to decipher the emotional signals of those around you, feeling like you're reading a language you don't quite understand? You're not alone. We're all on a journey to understand the intricate world of emotions, a journey that leads us to the heart of emotional literacy.

Emotional literacy isn't just about knowing the difference between happy and sad. It's about understanding the why behind the feelings, the subtle shifts in our inner weather, and how to navigate those shifts with grace and skill. It's about becoming fluent in the language of the heart, both our own and others.

The Brain's Emotional Orchestra:

Imagine your brain as a complex orchestra, with different sections contributing to the symphony of your emotions. Neuroscience has given us a front-row seat to this performance, revealing the intricate interplay of brain structures and chemicals that shape our emotional lives.

The Amygdala: The Fire Alarm: This little almond-shaped powerhouse acts like a vigilant fire alarm, constantly scanning the environment for potential threats. It's quick to trigger the "fight-or-flight" response, ensuring our survival in the face of danger. But sometimes, it can be a bit overzealous, sounding the alarm when there's no real fire.

The Hippocampus: The Memory Weaver: Like a skilled weaver, the hippocampus intertwines our emotional experiences with memories, creating a rich tapestry of associations. This is why a particular song can transport you back to a specific moment in time, flooding you with the emotions you felt then.

The Hypothalamus: The Body Conductor: This tiny but mighty conductor translates emotional signals into physiological responses. When we're scared, it cues the release of adrenaline, making our hearts race and our palms sweat. It's the reason we feel butterflies in our stomach before a big presentation.

The Prefrontal Cortex: The Wise Counselor: The prefrontal cortex, the brain's control center, steps in to regulate the emotional storm. It's the voice of reason, helping us to manage our impulses and make thoughtful decisions, even when our emotions are running high.

The Chemical Messengers: Neurotransmitters like serotonin and dopamine, and hormones like cortisol, act as chemical messengers, influencing our mood, motivation, and stress response. They're the secret ingredients in the emotional cocktail that shapes our experience.

The Vagus Nerve: The Calming Breath: The vagus nerve, a winding pathway connecting the brain to various organs, plays a crucial role in emotional regulation. It's like a gentle hand on the heart, helping to soothe us after a stressful experience. Deep breathing and mindfulness practices can activate this calming pathway.

Why Emotional Literacy Matters:

Emotional literacy isn't just a nice-to-have, it's a must-have for a fulfilling life. It's the foundation for mental well-being, strong relationships, and wise decision-making.

A Shield Against Stress: When we understand our emotions, we're better equipped to manage stress and bounce back from adversity. We can identify our triggers, develop healthy coping mechanisms, and prevent emotional overwhelm.

Building Bridges of Connection: Emotional literacy allows us to connect with others on a deeper level. It fosters empathy, helping us to understand and respond to the emotions of those around us, strengthening our relationships and reducing conflict.

Navigating the Crossroads of Choice: Emotions play a powerful role in our decision-making. Emotional literacy helps us to recognize how our feelings are influencing our choices, allowing us to make more informed and balanced decisions.

Unveiling the Self: Emotional literacy is a journey of self-discovery. It helps us to understand our own emotional landscape, recognizing our strengths, weaknesses, and patterns of behavior. This self-awareness is the key to personal growth and development.

The Art of Resilience: Life throws curveballs. Emotional literacy equips us with the resilience we need to weather the storms, learn from our experiences, and emerge stronger on the other side.

Cultivating Emotional Intelligence:

Emotional literacy is a skill, not an innate talent. It's something we can cultivate and refine throughout our lives.

   Naming the Feeling: The first step is to identify and name our emotions. Pay attention to your physical sensations, thoughts, and feelings. Keep a journal to track your emotional patterns.

   Expressing with Care: Expressing emotions in a healthy way is essential. Find constructive outlets for your feelings, whether it's talking to a trusted friend, writing, or engaging in creative pursuits.

   Mastering Regulation: Emotional regulation is about managing and modulating our emotional responses. Explore different coping strategies, such as mindfulness, deep breathing, or cognitive reappraisal.

   Walking in Another's Shoes: Empathy is the heart of emotional literacy. Practice actively listening to others, trying to understand their perspective, and being sensitive to their emotional needs.

   The Power of Presence: Mindfulness, the practice of being present without judgment, can be a powerful tool for developing emotional literacy. It allows us to observe our emotions without getting swept away by them.

   Seeking Guidance: If you're struggling with emotional challenges, don't hesitate to seek professional help. A therapist can provide guidance and support in developing emotional literacy skills.

Stories of Transformation:

The Stressed-Out Student: A college student overwhelmed by exam anxiety learns to identify the physical symptoms of her stress, understand its triggers, and develop relaxation techniques. She's able to manage her anxiety and improve her academic performance.

The Disconnected Couple: A couple struggling with communication learns to express their feelings more clearly and empathize with each other's perspectives. They rebuild their connection and create a more loving and supportive relationship.

The Grieving Heart: A person experiencing the loss of a loved one learns to process their grief in a healthy way, finding support and meaning in their experience. They discover their inner strength and resilience.

The Journey Continues:

Emotional literacy is a lifelong journey. It's a continuous process of learning, growing, and deepening our understanding of ourselves and others. As we become more fluent in the language of emotions, we unlock the potential for greater well-being, stronger relationships, and a more meaningful life. The journey may be challenging at times, but the rewards are immeasurable.

The Heart of Connection: Why Empathy Isn't Just Nice, It's Essential

Empathy. It's a word we hear a lot, but do we truly understand its power? It's more than just "putting yourself in someone else's shoes." It's about climbing into those shoes, walking a mile, and genuinely feeling the pinch of their experiences. In our increasingly complex world, empathy isn't a soft skill—it's the bedrock of meaningful connection, the key to navigating conflict, and the very lifeblood of strong, thriving relationships.

Think of empathy as a bridge. It spans the chasm between our individual realities, allowing us to glimpse the world through another's eyes. It's not just intellectual understanding; it's a visceral, emotional resonance. It's feeling the tremor of their sadness, the spark of their joy, as if it were your own. This shared emotional landscape fosters a depth of connection that transcends surface-level interactions.

Intimacy: The Delicate Dance of Vulnerability

Intimacy, that precious feeling of closeness, blossoms in the fertile ground of mutual understanding. Empathy is the sunshine that nurtures it. When we feel truly seen and heard, when we know someone genuinely cares about our inner world, we feel safe enough to shed our protective layers and reveal our authentic selves. This vulnerability, this courageous act of opening our hearts, is the gateway to profound intimacy.

Imagine this: Your partner comes home after a grueling day, their shoulders slumped, their spirit dimmed. A non-empathetic response might be, "You're always in a bad mood after work." Ouch. That's a wall builder. An empathetic response, however, might be, "You seem really drained. Rough day?" That's a bridge builder. It acknowledges their emotional state, opening a pathway for them to share their experience and for you to offer comfort. Empathy allows us to see beyond the surface behavior and connect with the emotions simmering beneath. It lets us celebrate each other's triumphs with genuine enthusiasm and offer solace in times of sorrow, weaving a tapestry of shared experiences that strengthens the bonds between us.

Conflict: From Battleground to Common Ground

Conflict is an inevitable part of human interaction. But empathy can transform a potential battleground into an opportunity for growth and understanding. Without empathy, conflict becomes a tug-of-war, each side digging in their heels, blinded by their own perspective. Empathy, however, provides a crucial detour. It encourages us to step outside our own viewpoint and try to understand the other person's reality, even if we don't agree with it.

Picture roommates clashing over chores. Without empathy, accusations fly, resentment festers. With empathy, one roommate might ask, "I've noticed you haven't been able to do your share lately. Is everything alright?" Perhaps the other roommate is swamped with work or dealing with a personal crisis. Understanding their context allows for a collaborative solution, like adjusting the chore schedule or offering support. Empathy isn't about condoning behavior; it's about understanding the "why" behind it, paving the way for constructive dialogue and compromise.

Relationships: The Tapestry of Human Connection

Strong relationships are woven with threads of respect, trust, and understanding—all spun from the raw material of empathy. When we feel truly understood, trust deepens. When our feelings are respected, we reciprocate that respect. Empathy creates a virtuous cycle, where understanding breeds trust, and trust strengthens connection.

Empathy also fosters a sense of belonging, that fundamental human need to feel connected and accepted. When we know others genuinely care, we feel woven into the fabric of the relationship. This sense of belonging nourishes our souls and provides a safe harbor in the storms of life. Furthermore, empathy fuels prosocial behavior. When we resonate with another's feelings, we're more likely to offer help, show compassion, and simply be present for them. These acts of kindness, big and small, reinforce the bonds that tie us together.

Empathy in Action: Real-World Stories

   The Healing Touch: A doctor, instead of rushing through a diagnosis, sits with a frightened patient, listens to their fears, and acknowledges their anxieties. This empathetic approach builds trust and improves the patient's well-being.

   Bridging the Divide: Two colleagues disagree on a project. One takes the time to understand the other's perspective, leading to a collaborative solution that incorporates the best of both ideas.

   Nurturing a Teen's Heart: A parent senses their teenager is struggling. Instead of dismissing it as "teenage angst," they listen with an open heart, creating a safe space for their child to share their burdens.

Cultivating Empathy: A Journey Worth Taking

Empathy isn't an innate trait; it's a skill we can cultivate. Here are some tools for your empathy toolkit:

   Listen Actively: Truly listen, not just waiting for your turn to speak. Pay attention to both words and body language.

Seek Perspectives: Make a conscious effort to see things from the other person's point of view. Ask yourself, "What might they be experiencing?"

Tune into Emotions: Become more aware of your own emotions and how they influence your interactions. This self-awareness will help you understand others' emotions.

Practice Compassion: Engage in practices that foster compassion, like mindfulness meditation.

Explore Diverse Worlds: Connect with people from different backgrounds and cultures to broaden your understanding of human experience.

Immerse Yourself in Stories: Reading fiction and watching films can expand your capacity for empathy by allowing you to connect with characters and their journeys.

Empathy is a lifelong journey, a continuous unfolding. By actively nurturing this capacity within ourselves, we not only enrich our own lives but also contribute to a more compassionate and interconnected world. In a world often fractured by division, empathy is the bridge we desperately need, the key to building a more harmonious and understanding future. It's not just nice; it's necessary.

Unlocking the Power of Connection: Mastering Communication

Let's face it, communication isn't just about slinging words at each other. It's the lifeblood of our relationships, the engine of our success, and the very fabric of how we connect with the world. It's messy, beautiful, and often frustrating, but when we get it right, it's magic. This section dives into the art of truly hearing and being heard, exploring active listening, assertiveness, and the transformative power of nonviolent communication.

3.3.1 Tuning In: The Art of Active Listening

Imagine a world where everyone felt truly heard. No more surface-level chatter, just genuine connection. That's the promise of active listening. It's not a passive activity; it's a full-body, full-mind commitment to understanding another human being.

Think of it like this: You're not just listening to the words, you're listening to the music behind them. The unspoken emotions, the subtle cues, the story the speaker is trying to tell.

Here's your active listening toolkit:

Laser Focus: Ditch the distractions – your phone, your racing thoughts, the squirrel outside the window. Make eye contact (but not in a creepy way!), nod, lean in. Show them they have your undivided attention.

Curiosity is Key: Ask questions! Not to interrupt, but to understand. "Tell me more about that," or "What was that like for you?" are great starting points. Think of yourself as a detective, gently probing to uncover the whole story.

Mirror, Mirror: Reflect back what you're hearing. "So, if I'm getting this right, you're saying…?" This not only confirms your understanding but also shows the speaker you're paying attention.

Walk in Their Shoes: Empathy isn't agreement; it's understanding. Try to see the situation from their perspective, even if you don't agree with it. A simple "I can see why you'd feel that way" can go a long way.

Hold Your Horses: Resist the urge to jump in with your own story or advice. Let them finish their thought. Your time to contribute will come, but first, truly listen.

No Judgment Zone: Suspend your inner critic. Focus on understanding their message, not judging it.

Meaningful Feedback: Once they're done, offer thoughtful feedback. Summarize their main points, ask clarifying questions, or share your own perspective respectfully.

Active Listening in Real Life:

Scenario: Your teammate is venting about a difficult client. Instead of tuning them out, make eye contact, nod, and say, 'That sounds incredibly frustrating. What's been the most challenging part?"

Scenario: Your friend is sharing some exciting news. Don't just offer a quick "congrats." Ask them about the details, how they're feeling, and what it means to them.

The Ripple Effect:

Active listening isn't just good manners; it's a game-changer. Studies show that it improves team performance, reduces conflict, and strengthens relationships. When people feel heard, they feel valued, and that makes all the difference.

3.3.2 Standing Your Ground: The Power of Assertiveness

Assertiveness isn't about being aggressive or passive; it's about finding that sweet spot in the middle where you can express your needs and opinions respectfully. It's about owning your voice without stepping on anyone else's toes.

The Assertiveness Arsenal:

"I" Statements: These are your secret weapon. Instead of "You always interrupt me," try "I feel frustrated when I'm interrupted because I have important information to share."

Clarity is King: Be specific about what you want or need. Vague requests lead to vague results.

Respectful Tone: Even when disagreeing, maintain a calm and respectful tone. Think confident, not confrontational.

Boundary Patrol: Setting boundaries is essential. It's okay to say "no" to things that don't align with your priorities or well-being.

Solutions, Not Just Problems: When raising a concern, try to offer a constructive solution. This shows you're not just complaining, you're invested in finding a positive outcome.

Persistence Pays Off: Sometimes, you'll need to be persistent. Don't give up easily, but always remain respectful.

Assertiveness in Action:

Scenario: You need to decline a meeting invitation. Instead of making excuses, say, "Thank you for the invitation. I won't be able to attend as I have another commitment, but I'm happy to catch up afterward."

Scenario: You need to give constructive feedback to a colleague. Instead of saying "You did this wrong," try "I noticed that the report was missing some key data. Would you be open to discussing how we can ensure it's more comprehensive next time?"

The Confidence Boost:

Assertiveness empowers you to take control of your communication and your life. It builds confidence, strengthens relationships, and helps you achieve your goals.

3.3.3 Speaking from the Heart: The Magic of Nonviolent Communication

Nonviolent Communication (NVC), developed by Marshall Rosenberg, takes communication to a deeper level. It's about connecting with compassion and understanding, even in the midst of conflict. It's about speaking from the heart and listening with empathy.

The NVC Recipe:

Observe: Describe the situation without judgment. Just the facts.
Feel: Express your feelings about the situation. Use "I" statements.
Need: Identify the underlying need that's connected to your feelings.
Request: Make a clear and specific request.

The NVC Mindset:

Empathy is Everything: Strive to understand others' feelings and needs, even when you disagree with them.
Honesty without Blame: Express yourself honestly without blaming or judging others.
Compassion in Action: Approach every interaction with compassion and understanding.
No Judgment Zone: Suspend judgment and focus on connecting with the other person.

NVC in Real Life:

Scenario: Your roommate hasn't done their share of the chores. Instead of saying "You're so lazy," try "I've noticed that the dishes haven't been done for a few days (observation). I feel frustrated because I value a clean and tidy living space (feelings/needs). Would you be willing to take on dish duty this week? (request)."

Scenario: You're in a heated discussion with a family member. Instead of getting defensive, try saying "I'm feeling really stressed right now (feeling). I need to feel heard and understood (need). Can we take a break and come back to this later when we're both calmer? (request)."

The Power of Connection:

NVC is a powerful tool for building stronger, more compassionate relationships. It helps us understand ourselves and others on a deeper level, leading to greater connection and understanding. It's not always easy, but the rewards are immeasurable.

Taming the Inner Storm: Emotional Regulation for Thriving Relationships

Let's be honest, life throws curveballs. Stress, like a persistent drizzle, can dampen even the most vibrant relationships. It seeps into our interactions, turning molehills into mountains and whispers into shouts. But here's the good news: we're not helpless passengers on this emotional rollercoaster. We can learn to navigate these turbulent times with grace and skill, fostering stronger, more resilient connections. It's all about emotional regulation – learning to understand and manage our feelings so they don't hijack our relationships.

Think of your emotions as a powerful, sometimes unruly, horse. Left unchecked, it can bolt, dragging you and your loved ones into a chaotic mess. Emotional regulation is like learning to ride that horse, understanding its temperament, and guiding it with a steady hand. It's not about suppressing emotions; it's about understanding them, acknowledging them, and responding in ways that nurture, rather than damage, our relationships.

When Stress Knocks at the Door:

Stress is a relationship's kryptonite. It shrinks our capacity for empathy, turning us into reactive, short-fused versions of ourselves. Suddenly, small annoyances become epic battles. We misinterpret our partner's innocent comments as personal attacks, and the cycle of negativity begins.

Communication Catastrophe: Stress muzzles our communication. We struggle to articulate our needs, our listening skills vanish, and we become masters of misinterpretation. Imagine trying to build a house while everyone speaks a different language – that's what stressed communication feels like.

Intimacy Evaporation: Stress sucks the oxygen out of intimacy. When we're consumed by worries, we have little emotional energy left for connection. Physical affection dwindles, shared laughter fades, and meaningful conversations become rare. We become strangers in our own homes.

Conflict Bonanza: Stress is a conflict amplifier. It turns minor disagreements into full-blown wars. Our problem-solving skills take a vacation, leaving us stuck in a cycle of blame and resentment.

The Spillover Effect: Stress doesn't stay neatly compartmentalized. It has a way of leaking into every area of our lives. A bad day at work can translate into a tense evening at home, poisoning the atmosphere with negativity.

The Long Haul: Chronic stress is a relationship killer. It erodes trust, fuels resentment, and can ultimately lead to separation or divorce. It's a slow drip that can eventually erode even the strongest foundations.

Reclaiming Control: Strategies for Emotional Mastery:

So, how do we tame this emotional beast? Here are some powerful tools for building emotional regulation skills:

Know Thyself (and Thy Triggers): Self-awareness is the bedrock of emotional regulation. Understanding what triggers your emotional responses is crucial. Are you a pressure cooker that explodes under deadlines? Do you retreat into your shell when feeling criticized? Journaling, meditation, or even talking to a trusted friend can help you map your emotional landscape.

Mindfulness Magic: Mindfulness is like a pause button for your emotions. It allows you to observe your feelings without judgment, creating a space between your emotions and your reactions. Deep breathing, meditation, and simply paying attention to the present moment can work wonders.

Rewrite Your Narrative: Our thoughts shape our emotions. Cognitive restructuring helps us challenge negative thought patterns and replace them with more balanced perspectives. Instead of assuming the worst, we learn to consider alternative explanations.

Speak Your Truth (Respectfully): Effective communication is essential. Learning to express your needs and feelings assertively, without blaming or attacking, is key. "I" statements are your friend. "I feel hurt when..." is far less inflammatory than "You always make me feel..."

Conflict as an Opportunity: Conflict is inevitable, but it doesn't have to be destructive. Learning conflict resolution skills can help you navigate disagreements constructively, focusing on finding solutions rather than winning arguments.

Stress-Busting Strategies: Managing stress is non-negotiable. Identify your stress triggers and develop healthy coping mechanisms. Exercise, relaxation techniques, hobbies, and spending time in nature can all help.

Don't Go It Alone: Sometimes, we need a little help. Therapists and counselors can provide guidance and support, teaching evidence-based strategies for emotional regulation and conflict resolution.

Real-Life Transformations:

John and Sarah: Stressed and snapping at each other, John and Sarah learned to identify their stress triggers and communicate more effectively. They rediscovered intimacy through shared activities and learned to support each other through challenging times.

Maria and David: Conflict avoiders to the core, Maria and David learned to face their fears and address disagreements constructively. They discovered that open communication, even when uncomfortable, brought them closer.

The Ripple Effect:

Emotional regulation isn't just about personal well-being; it has a ripple effect on the world around us. When we learn to manage our emotions, we create healthier relationships, stronger families, and more compassionate communities. It's a gift we give not only to ourselves but to everyone we touch. So, let's embrace the journey of emotional mastery, one breath, one conversation, one mindful moment at a time.

Part 2: Building Foundations for Enduring Partnerships

Redefining Romance: Love and Connection in the 21st Century

Beyond the Fireworks: Why Everyday Love Makes a Relationship Glow

We've all seen the movies: the flash mob proposal, the surprise trip to a tropical paradise, the diamond ring the size of a small car. Grand romantic gestures? They're dazzling, sure. They create fireworks. But what happens after the last firework fades? What keeps the relationship glowing, not just sparkling for a night? That's where the magic of everyday romance comes in. It's the quiet hum of love, not the explosive boom, that truly powers a lasting connection.

Think of it this way: grand gestures are like vacations – amazing, but temporary. Everyday romance is like having a cozy, loving home. You can't live on vacations alone. It's the small, consistent acts of love, the little "I'm thinking of you" moments woven into the fabric of daily life, that build a relationship you truly want to come home to. It's not just about feeling love; it's about living it, one tiny, thoughtful action at a time.

The Science of Snuggles (and Other Small Things):

There's real psychology behind this. We humans are wired for connection. Those little acts of kindness? They're like tiny love notes to the brain. They whisper, "You're valued.

You're seen. You matter." This builds a sense of security, a feeling of being deeply understood, which is the bedrock of intimacy. Think of it as filling up your partner's "love bank" with small deposits of affection. When life throws curveballs (and it always does), you'll have that reserve of positive feelings to draw on.

Psychologists who study relationships keep finding the same thing: it's the frequency of positive interactions, not just the intensity of the grand gestures, that predicts relationship success. It's like tending a garden. You can't just throw a bunch of fertilizer on it once a year and expect it to thrive. You need to nurture it regularly, day in and day out.

Love in Action: A Pocketful of Everyday Magic:

The beauty of everyday romance is that it's personal. It's about knowing your partner and expressing love in ways that speak directly to their heart. Here are a few ideas to get you started:

The Language of Touch: A gentle squeeze of the hand, a playful nudge, a lingering hug – these small physical connections speak volumes. They release oxytocin, the "cuddle hormone," which strengthens our bonds.

Acts of Service (aka, Love in Overalls): Doing the dishes when your partner is swamped, picking up their dry cleaning, making their morning coffee just the way they like it – these practical gestures say, "I see you, I care about you, and I want to make your life a little easier."

Words that Warm the Heart: A genuine compliment, a heartfelt "thank you," a simple "I love you" whispered at just the right moment – words have power. They can lift spirits, boost confidence, and make your partner feel truly cherished.

Time Well Spent (Not Just "Spent" Together): Putting down your phone and truly listening when your partner talks, sharing a laugh over a silly meme, cuddling on the couch while watching a movie – these moments of focused attention create memories and deepen intimacy.

Little Surprises, Big Impact: Bringing home their favorite treat, leaving a sweet note on their mirror, sending them a funny text during the day – these small, unexpected gestures show that they're on your mind.

The Art of Active Listening: Really listening, without interrupting or judging, is a powerful act of love. It says, "Your thoughts and feelings matter to me."

Real Love Stories (Because Life Isn't a Rom-Com):

The Long Haul: One couple, married for 50 years, told me their secret: they still hold hands while watching TV. It's a small thing, but it's a constant reminder of their connection.

The Balancing Act: A busy couple with kids carves out "mini-dates" – 15 minutes of uninterrupted conversation each evening. It's their way of staying connected amidst the chaos.

The Comeback Story: After a difficult period, one couple rediscovered their love through small acts of kindness. He started making her breakfast every morning. She started leaving him encouraging notes. These little things helped them rebuild their trust and intimacy.

Keeping the Flame Alive (Because Life Happens):

Let's be real, life gets in the way. Stress, work, family – it's easy to let those little acts of love slide. But remember:

Talk About It: Communication is key. What makes your partner feel loved? Ask them! And be honest about what makes you feel loved too.

Be Consistent: One grand gesture a year won't cut it. It's the small, consistent actions that make the difference.

Be Flexible: Relationships change, and so do people's needs. Be willing to adapt your expressions of love as your relationship evolves.

Take Care of Yourself: You can't pour from an empty cup. Make sure you're taking care of your own well-being so you have the energy to nurture your relationship.

The Future of Connection:

In our fast-paced, digital world, the need for genuine connection is greater than ever. Everyday romance isn't some outdated idea; it's the key to building meaningful, lasting relationships. It's about slowing down, paying attention, and showing your love not just in grand gestures, but in the quiet, everyday moments that make a life together truly beautiful. It's not about fireworks; it's about the steady, warm glow of a love that lasts.

Love Languages in 2025: A Heart-to-Heart

Forget the dusty rulebook. Let's talk about love, not as a rigid set of boxes, but as the vibrant, ever-shifting dance it truly is. Gary Chapman's five love languages gave us a great starting point, a way to begin the conversation, but love in 2025 is so much more nuanced, so much more human than a simple quiz.

Think of it like this: love isn't a single instrument playing one note. It's a whole orchestra, a symphony of connection. And just like a musician might play several instruments beautifully, we all have a range of "love dialects," some we speak more fluently than others.

The Familiar Five: A Quick Refresher (with a 2025 twist)

Words of Affirmation: Still powerful, but now amplified by technology. A quick "I'm thinking of you" text can be a tiny love bomb. A public shout-out on social media? Maybe not everyone's cup of tea. It's about knowing the person, not just the language.

Acts of Service: In our hyper-busy world, these acts are more precious than ever. It's not just about chores; it's about anticipating needs, showing you see them. Picking up takeout after a long day? Pure gold.

Receiving Gifts: It's not the thing itself, but the thought that counts. A quirky little something that shows you get them? That's the magic. A personalized playlist? Way more meaningful than another generic gift card.

Quality Time: In a world of constant distraction, undivided attention is the ultimate luxury. Putting down your phone, truly listening – that's where the connection deepens. It's not just about being together, but truly being present.

Physical Touch: From a gentle squeeze of the hand to a full-on bear hug, touch speaks volumes. But it's about knowing the right touch, the kind that makes them feel safe and loved, not uncomfortable.

Beyond the Five: Where Love Gets Interesting

Here's where things get juicy. Love isn't confined to five neat little categories. It's messy, it's fluid, it's beautifully unpredictable.

Love is Contextual: Our "love language" might change depending on who we're with, what's going on in our lives. We might crave words of affirmation from our boss, acts of service from our stressed-out partner, and physical touch from our kids.

Love is Personal: We're all unique snowflakes. Some of us express love through shared hobbies, intellectual sparring, or even just giving each other space to breathe. It's about understanding the individual, not forcing them into a pre-defined box.

Love is Cultural: A hug might be a common greeting in one culture, a deeply intimate gesture in another. Understanding these cultural nuances is essential, especially in our increasingly interconnected world.

Love is for Everyone: Neurodiversity reminds us that love expresses itself in countless ways. What looks like "aloofness" might be a different way of showing affection. It's about opening our hearts and minds to the infinite variety of human connection.

Love is Digital: In 2025, our online and offline lives are intertwined. A thoughtful meme, a shared playlist, a virtual movie night – these are all valid expressions of love in the digital age.

Love Starts with Self: How do you show yourself love? Do you treat yourself to a massage (physical touch)? Do you celebrate your accomplishments (words of affirmation)? Understanding your own "self-love language" is the foundation for healthy relationships with others.

Real Love Stories (not just textbook examples)

The Tech-Savvy Couple: They "speak" each other's love language through carefully curated playlists, shared memes, and late-night chats. It might look like they're always on their phones, but they're actually deeply connected.

The Quiet Couple: They don't shower each other with grand gestures. Their love is expressed in the comfortable silence they share, the way they anticipate each other's needs, the gentle touch of a hand on a shoulder.

The Long-Distance Lovers: They bridge the miles with daily video calls, surprise deliveries of their favorite treats, and heartfelt letters that arrive like precious gifts.

The Takeaway: Ditch the Labels, Embrace the Humanity

Love isn't about fitting people into neat little boxes. It's about seeing them, truly seeing them, with all their quirks and complexities. It's about listening, learning, and being willing to adapt. It's about celebrating the beautiful, messy, unpredictable dance of human connection. In 2025, let's move beyond the labels and embrace the infinite languages of love.

The Heart of Connection: Weaving Gratitude into the Fabric of Love

Love isn't just a feeling; it's a vibrant garden we cultivate together. And at the heart of that garden, blooming in rich colors, is appreciation. It's not simply good manners; it's the very air that nourishes a thriving relationship. This isn't about reciting thank-yous like a grocery list; it's about truly seeing your partner, recognizing the unique melody they bring to your shared song, and letting them know how much their music means to you.

Think of appreciation as a love language spoken not just with words, but with the quiet understanding in your eyes, the gentle touch of your hand, the shared laughter that bubbles up from a place of deep connection. It's about noticing the way their brow furrows when they're concentrating, the goofy grin that spreads across their face when they're genuinely happy, the quiet strength they show when life throws its curveballs. It's about cherishing these little details that make them them.

Why is appreciation so potent? Because it whispers, "You matter to me. I see you, not just as my partner, but as a unique and wonderful human being." It's a form of positive reinforcement, a gentle nudge that encourages those beautiful qualities to blossom even brighter. When we feel appreciated, we feel safe, loved, and understood. And when we feel safe, loved, and understood, we're more likely to open our hearts and connect on a deeper level.

Science backs this up, too. Studies show a clear link between expressed gratitude and happier, healthier relationships. Couples who regularly voice their appreciation report higher levels of satisfaction, intimacy, and commitment. Gratitude acts like a shield against negativity, softening the edges of disagreements and fostering a spirit of understanding. It's not just good for the relationship; it's good for you. Expressing gratitude has been shown to boost our own well-being, reducing stress and bringing a sense of joy.

So, how do we weave more appreciation into our daily lives? It's less about grand gestures and more about the small, consistent acts of recognition. Did they make your coffee just the way you like it? Tell them! Did they listen patiently while you vented about your day? Thank them, genuinely. Did they just make you laugh until your sides hurt? Let them know how much you cherish those moments.

Be Specific: Instead of a generic "Thanks," try, "I really appreciate you taking out the trash. It makes my life so much easier."

Make it a Habit: Find little ways to express gratitude every day. A quick text, a handwritten note, a spontaneous hug – these small gestures can speak volumes.

Use "I" Statements: "I feel so loved when you..." or "I really appreciate it when you..." makes your gratitude more personal and impactful.

Show, Don't Just Tell: Sometimes, actions speak louder than words. Surprise them with a thoughtful gift, plan a date night, or simply offer to help with a task they've been struggling with.

Create a Ritual: Maybe it's sharing three things you're grateful for about each other before bed, or starting a "gratitude jar" where you jot down little notes of appreciation.

Imagine a couple, Emily and Ben, who were drifting apart. Through therapy, they realized they'd stopped seeing each other. They'd fallen into a routine, taking each other for granted. They started small, with Emily thanking Ben for making her laugh and Ben expressing his gratitude for Emily's unwavering support. Slowly, the warmth returned to their relationship. They started seeing each other again, not just as roommates, but as lovers, friends, and partners in this beautiful dance of life.

Appreciation is the lifeblood of a healthy relationship. It's the gentle rain that nourishes the seeds of love, allowing them to grow and flourish. It's not a one-time fix, but a continuous practice, a conscious choice to see the good in your partner and let them know how much they mean to you. And in doing so, you not only strengthen your bond but also enrich your own life with a deeper sense of joy and gratitude.

Weaving Tapestries of Togetherness: The Art of Shared Experiences

Ever notice how some memories cling to us, vibrant and warm, while others fade like old photographs? Often, the most vivid recollections are those interwoven with shared laughter, whispered secrets, and the simple joy of experiencing something alongside someone we care about. These aren't just memories; they're the building blocks of connection, the very essence of what makes relationships flourish. Let's explore this fascinating landscape of shared experiences and discover how they shape the bonds that enrich our lives.

The Human Need for "We": A Journey into Connection

Deep down, we're all social creatures. It's in our DNA, a primal urge to connect, to belong. Think back to our ancestors: sharing a hunt, weathering a storm together – these shared struggles and triumphs forged bonds crucial for survival. This inherent drive for connection echoes in our modern lives, manifesting in our desire for companionship, shared laughter, and the creation of stories we can tell together.

Shared experiences aren't just pleasant; they're psychologically powerful. They contribute to stronger, longer-lasting relationships through a beautiful interplay of factors:

The "Happy Hormone" Cocktail: Remember that exhilarating feeling after a roller coaster ride or the warm glow after a shared accomplishment? That's the magic of endorphins at work! Enjoyable activities release these feel-good chemicals, creating positive associations with the person you're sharing the experience with. That shared joy becomes intertwined with your memory of them, strengthening the attraction and connection.

Unlocking the Heart's Secrets: Imagine navigating a bustling market in a foreign city together. The shared adventure can spark conversations you wouldn't have otherwise. These moments of vulnerability, of revealing your true self to another, build trust and intimacy. It's like slowly unfolding the layers of a precious map, revealing the hidden treasures within.

The Power of "Us": Shared experiences cultivate a sense of interdependence, that comforting feeling of knowing you're not alone. Working towards a common goal, whether it's training for a marathon or simply assembling a particularly tricky piece of furniture, strengthens the feeling of "we-ness." It's like building a raft together, knowing you'll navigate the rapids more effectively as a team.

Crafting a Shared Narrative: As you collect shared experiences, you begin to weave a unique tapestry of "your story" together. These experiences become part of your shared identity, shaping how you see yourselves as a couple, a family, or a group of friends. It's like writing a book together, each chapter filled with shared adventures and inside jokes.

The Memory Vault: Shared experiences tend to stick with us longer than solo ones. Reminiscing, looking through photos, and retelling stories reinforces the emotional connection. These shared memories become a treasure trove of positive moments, a source of comfort and strength during challenging times.

From Cozy Nights to Grand Adventures: The Spectrum of Shared Experiences

The beauty of shared experiences lies in their diversity. It's not about the scale, but the heart behind them.

The Quiet Magic of Everyday Moments: Don't underestimate the power of the small things. Sharing a quiet cup of coffee in the morning, laughing at a silly meme together, or simply holding hands during a walk – these seemingly insignificant moments create a sense of closeness and connection that builds over time.

Shared Passions, Shared Joy: Engaging in hobbies and interests you both love creates opportunities for fun, learning, and shared laughter. Whether it's painting, hiking, or geeking out over the latest sci-fi novel, shared passions create common ground and foster camaraderie.

Embracing the Unknown, Together: Stepping outside your comfort zone and facing challenges together can be incredibly bonding. Traveling to a new place, learning a new skill, or tackling a difficult project can create a sense of shared accomplishment and strengthen your resilience as a team.

The Rhythm of Rituals and Traditions: Creating shared rituals, like celebrating birthdays with specific traditions or having a weekly game night, provides a sense of continuity and strengthens your bond. These rituals become cherished memories, passed down through generations, creating a sense of belonging.

Sharing Life's Ups and Downs: Being there for each other through thick and thin, celebrating milestones, and offering support during tough times are essential for building strong relationships. These shared experiences create a sense of shared history and foster deep empathy and understanding.

Shared Visions: The Power of Values and Goals

Finding Your North Star: Why Shared Values Are the Heart of Strong Relationships

Ever feel like you're wandering through life without a map, especially when it comes to relationships? The truth is, a strong connection, whether with a romantic partner, family, or friend, needs a shared sense of direction – a "life compass" guided by aligned values. Think of it as the invisible glue that binds you together, creating a foundation of mutual respect, understanding, and unwavering support, even when life throws curveballs. Without this shared understanding of what truly matters, relationships can crumble under the weight of misunderstandings and friction.

Let's unpack this idea of a "life compass" a bit more. It's woven from three interconnected threads: values, beliefs, and life goals. They're all distinct, yet they influence each other in fascinating ways.

Values: These are the deep-seated principles that shape our choices and actions. They're the "why" behind what we do. Honesty, compassion, creativity, loyalty – these are just a few examples. Values act as a filter, influencing how we see the world and make decisions. They're the core of who we are.

Beliefs: These are our convictions about the world, often shaped by our experiences, upbringing, and culture. They can range from religious or political views to personal philosophies about success or happiness. Beliefs are the stories we tell ourselves about how the world works.

Life Goals: These are the milestones we aim for, often inspired by our values and beliefs. They can be anything from starting a family to climbing the corporate ladder, traveling the world, or making a difference in our community. Life goals give us something to strive for, a sense of purpose.

These three elements are in constant interplay. Our values shape our beliefs, and together, they guide the life goals we set. For example, someone who values creativity and believes in the power of self-expression might dream of becoming a musician. Someone who values security and believes in financial stability might prioritize a career in finance.

So, why are shared values so crucial for relationships? Imagine two ships sailing in the same direction – they're far less likely to collide. Shared values create that same sense of direction in relationships, leading to:

Deeper Understanding: When you share values, you speak the same language, making it easier to see where the other person is coming from, even when you disagree. You understand their motivations because you share similar priorities.

Open Communication: Shared values create a safe space for honest and open dialogue. You feel comfortable sharing your thoughts and feelings without fear of judgment because you know you're on the same wavelength.

Rock-Solid Trust: Knowing that someone shares your fundamental principles builds trust and respect. It creates a sense of security and allows for deeper intimacy.

Smoother Conflict Resolution: Disagreements are inevitable, but when you share core values, you can navigate conflicts more constructively. You can approach disagreements with a shared understanding of what's truly important, making it easier to find solutions that work for both of you.

Happier, More Fulfilling Relationships: Research consistently shows that shared values are linked to greater relationship satisfaction. When you're on the same page about what matters most, it creates a sense of harmony and shared purpose, contributing to overall well-being.

Lasting Bonds: Relationships built on shared values are more likely to weather life's storms. When challenges arise, those shared values act as an anchor, providing stability and resilience.

It's important to remember that it's not just about having identical values; it's about perceiving that you share similar values. Open communication is key to understanding each other's perspectives and recognizing the values you hold in common.

And remember, values can evolve over time. Regularly checking in with each other and discussing how your values might have shifted is essential for maintaining a strong connection.

While perfect alignment isn't always possible, and some degree of difference is natural, focusing on the core values that are non-negotiable is crucial. Open communication, mutual respect, and a willingness to compromise are essential for navigating any differences.

Think of cultivating shared values as tending a garden. It requires conscious effort, but the rewards are immeasurable. By exploring each other's values, sharing experiences that align with those values, and creating a safe space for open dialogue, you can nurture a relationship that thrives on a foundation of shared purpose and understanding. It's an investment in a future filled with deeper connection, greater happiness, and a love that truly lasts.

Bridging the Divide: When Worlds Collide (and How to Embrace the Spark)

Let's face it, navigating the choppy waters of differing worldviews can feel like trying to build a sandcastle during a hurricane. Whether it's your partner's staunchly held political beliefs clashing with your own, or family dinners turning into battlegrounds over religion, these deeply rooted differences can feel like an insurmountable chasm. But what if, instead of fearing the divide, we saw it as an opportunity to build a bridge?

Think of worldviews as intricate tapestries, woven with threads of upbringing, experiences, and beliefs. They're the lenses through which we interpret the world, coloring our perceptions of right and wrong, and shaping our very identities. So, when these tapestries clash, it's not just a disagreement about politics or religion – it's a clash of fundamental perspectives. And in today's hyper-connected, often polarized world, these clashes seem to be happening more frequently, and with greater intensity.

It's tempting to retreat to our own corners, surrounding ourselves with echoes of our own beliefs. But true growth, both personally and in our relationships, lies in venturing beyond those comfortable boundaries. It's about daring to engage with perspectives that challenge us, not to convert or conquer, but to understand and connect.

So, how do we navigate this complex terrain? Think of it as a journey, not a destination. Here are a few tools to pack for the trip:

Active Listening: The Art of Truly Hearing: Forget about formulating your rebuttal while someone else is talking. Really listen. Not just to the words, but to the emotions behind them. Ask questions, not to trap, but to clarify. "I hear you saying X, and it sounds like that's important to you because Y." This simple act of acknowledgment can diffuse tension and open a pathway for genuine dialogue.

Empathy: Walking a Mile in Their Shoes (Even if You Disagree with Their Footwear): Empathy isn't about condoning someone's beliefs; it's about understanding their origins. Where did their perspective come from? What experiences shaped their worldview? Try to see the world through their eyes, even if just for a moment. "I may not agree with your stance on Z, but I can see how you arrived at that conclusion given your background."

Respectful Communication: Ditch the Swords, Grab the Words: Name-calling, personal attacks, and dismissive language have no place in constructive dialogue. Focus on expressing your own perspective clearly and respectfully, using "I" statements to avoid accusatory "you" statements. "I feel concerned about A because of B," is far less confrontational than, "You're wrong about A!"

Common Ground: Finding the Shared Soil: Even amidst a forest of differing opinions, there are often patches of shared ground. Perhaps you both value family, community, or justice, even if your paths to achieving those values diverge. Focus on these shared values, building a foundation for connection even when you disagree on the details.

Boundaries: Drawing Lines in the Sand (Respectfully): Not every topic is up for debate. Sometimes, the most loving thing you can do is agree to disagree. Identify those hot-button issues that consistently lead to unproductive conflict and respectfully declare them off-limits.

Seeking Common Goals: From Argument to Action: Instead of battling over abstract ideologies, find concrete ways to collaborate. Volunteer for a local cause, work on a community project, or simply find shared hobbies that transcend political or religious divides. Working together towards a common goal can foster connection and build bridges across seemingly insurmountable differences.

Emotional Triggers: Knowing Your Buttons (and Theirs): We all have emotional triggers – topics or phrases that can ignite a firestorm of emotion. Understanding your own triggers, and becoming aware of your partner's, can help you approach sensitive conversations with greater care and avoid accidentally pushing those buttons.

Taking Breaks: The Power of the Pause: When discussions become heated, it's okay to step away. A cooling-off period can allow both parties to regain composure and return to the conversation with fresh perspectives.

Relationship First: Love Over Logic (Sometimes): At the end of the day, the relationship is often more important than winning an argument. Be willing to compromise, to listen, and to prioritize connection over being right.

The world of relationships in 2025 is complex. Social media echo chambers and the fear of being "canceled" can make navigating differing worldviews even more challenging. But there's also a growing movement towards inclusivity and a recognition that understanding and empathy are essential for building a more harmonious society.

Navigating differences isn't about changing someone's mind; it's about building bridges of understanding. It's about recognizing our shared humanity, even in the face of profound disagreement. It's about embracing the spark of connection, even when worlds collide. And sometimes, it's about recognizing that love, respect, and understanding are more valuable than being right.

Weaving Dreams Together: The Art of Shared Futures

Ever feel like you and your partner are paddling in separate canoes, even though you're in the same river? That's where the magic of shared goals comes in. It's not about identical dreams, but about weaving your individual aspirations into a shared tapestry, creating a "we" that's stronger and more beautiful than two "I"s. Imagine building a house together, not just of bricks and mortar, but of shared memories and future laughter. That's the power we're talking about.

Think of shared goals as the North Star guiding your relationship. They're not just about the big milestones – buying a house, raising a family – but also the subtle, everyday things, like creating a home filled with joy or making a difference in your community. These shared visions act like glue, binding you together through thick and thin. When you're both invested in something bigger than yourselves, it deepens your commitment, gives you a sense of direction, and makes navigating life's bumps a whole lot easier. Plus, let's be honest, celebrating wins together? Pure joy.

But here's the secret sauce: shared goals don't mean sacrificing your own individuality. It's about finding the sweet spot where your dreams intertwine, where you cheer each other on, even when your paths diverge slightly. Imagine one partner dreaming of climbing Everest while the other yearns to write a novel. Supporting each other, celebrating small victories, offering a shoulder to lean on – that's the kindling that keeps the fire of your relationship burning bright.

So, how do you actually do this? It starts with honest, open conversations. Think of it as a brainstorming session for your future, no idea too wild or unrealistic. Grab some coffee, light a candle, and just talk. What do you both truly want? What makes your hearts sing? Don't be afraid to be vulnerable, to share those secret dreams you've tucked away.

Once you've got a sense of your shared vision, start turning those dreams into concrete goals. Think SMART: Specific, Measurable, Achievable, Relevant, and Time-bound. "Travel the world" is a lovely sentiment, but "backpack through Southeast Asia for three weeks in two years" is a plan you can actually work with. And remember, plans aren't set in stone. Life throws curveballs, so be flexible, be willing to adjust, and keep checking in with each other.

Supporting individual dreams is just as vital. It's about being your partner's biggest cheerleader, offering practical help, and creating space for them to pursue their passions. Maybe it's driving them to a class, proofreading their work, or just giving them a quiet evening to focus. Small gestures, big impact.

Let's paint a picture. Imagine a couple who dream of opening a bakery. They work together on the business plan, divide responsibilities, and taste-test countless recipes (yum!). That's their shared goal. But she also loves pottery, and he's passionate about photography. They encourage each other, celebrate each other's creations, and maybe even find ways to blend their passions – gorgeous photos of her pottery displayed in the bakery.

Of course, there will be challenges. Priorities clash, disagreements arise, life throws you a loop. But with open communication, compromise, and a willingness to understand each other's perspectives, you can navigate these bumps in the road. Remember, you're a team.

Creating a shared future isn't a destination, it's a journey. It's about building a life together, brick by brick, dream by dream. It's about weaving your stories together, creating a masterpiece that reflects the unique beauty of your love. And that, my friends, is something truly special.

The Shifting Sands of "Us": Growing Together, Even When Life Pulls Us Apart

Let's be real, relationships aren't static. They're living, breathing things, just like us, constantly changing and evolving. Think of it less like a perfectly posed portrait and more like a dynamic, ever-shifting watercolor. This isn't just about the big, obvious stuff like weddings or buying a house. It's about the subtle shifts, the quiet growth spurts we experience as individuals, and how those ripples affect the "us" we've built. It's about navigating the sometimes-awkward, sometimes-exhilarating dance of growing together, even when life seems determined to pull us in different directions.

Life Throws Curveballs (and We Have to Catch Them Together):

Life has a funny way of throwing curveballs. One minute you're cruising along, comfortable in your routine, and the next, BAM! Career change, unexpected illness, a new baby (or an empty nest!), or maybe just the slow, steady shift of personal growth. These changes aren't just individual; they reverberate through the relationship, shaking things up and demanding adjustments. Think of it like a shared garden – if one plant suddenly grows taller and blocks the sun, the other needs to adapt or it won't thrive.

The Tightrope Walk of Change:

Navigating these changes as a couple can feel like walking a tightrope. Even "good" changes can bring stress. That dream promotion? Awesome! But also, longer hours and less time together. That adorable new baby? Joyful! But also, sleepless nights and a crash course in teamwork (often while running on fumes). It's easy for disconnects to happen. One partner might be sprinting ahead in one area while the other feels left behind, or maybe they're just processing things at different speeds.

The Danger Zones:

   Diverging Paths: Sometimes, you and your partner might find yourselves on different growth trajectories. One might be laser-focused on career, the other on personal development. It's not about judging which path is "better," but about making sure you're still walking together, even if the scenery looks different.
   Communication Blackouts: When stress hits, communication can be the first casualty. We clam up, we snap, we misinterpret. It's crucial to keep those lines of

communication open, even (and especially) when it feels hard.

Losing "Us": Big life changes can make us question our shared identity. The roles we used to play, the routines we cherished, might no longer fit. It's like redecorating a house – sometimes you have to let go of the old furniture to make room for the new.

The Uneven Load: Change often means redistributing responsibilities. If one partner feels like they're carrying more than their fair share, resentment can build. It's vital to have open conversations about fairness and adjust as needed.

Turning Tumbles into Triumphs:

But here's the good news: navigating change together can actually make your relationship stronger. It's like forging steel in fire – the heat can be intense, but the result is something incredibly resilient.

Deeper Connections: Vulnerability breeds intimacy. When you share your fears and hopes with your partner, you create a safe space for connection.

Building Resilience: Every challenge you overcome together strengthens your bond. You learn to rely on each other, to navigate rough patches, and to emerge stronger on the other side.

Reinventing "Us": Change is a chance to reimagine your relationship. It's an opportunity to explore new interests, set new goals, and create a future that excites you both.

Personal Growth, Shared Joy: When you support each other's individual growth, you both benefit. Your partner's successes become your successes, and their happiness adds to your own.

Real-Life Stories:

Sarah and Mark: Mark's career change was a rollercoaster. Initial excitement turned to financial strain and arguments. Therapy helped them communicate better and find solutions together. Ultimately, they learned to support each other's dreams, even when it was scary.

Emily and David: The empty nest left Emily and David feeling lost. Instead of dwelling on the past, they embraced the opportunity to reconnect. Dance classes, date nights, and rediscovering shared passions helped them fall in love all over again.

Tools for the Journey:

Talk it Out: Honest, open communication is key. Really listen to each other, even when it's uncomfortable.

Empathy is Your Superpower: Try to see things from your partner's perspective. Even if you don't agree, you can understand.

Flexibility is Your Friend: Life rarely goes according to plan. Be willing to adapt, compromise, and try new things.

Teamwork Makes the Dream Work: Approach challenges as a team, not as adversaries. Find solutions that work for both of you.

Don't Be Afraid to Ask for Help: Therapists, counselors, and even wise friends can offer valuable support.

Celebrate the Wins: Acknowledge and appreciate each other's efforts, both big and small.

Relationships in the 2025 Landscape:

In today's world, change is the only constant. We're living longer, redefining relationships, and breaking down traditional norms. This means couples need to be more adaptable, resilient, and communicative than ever before. It's not about finding a "perfect" balance, but about constantly adjusting and recalibrating as life throws its inevitable curveballs. It's about recognizing that "us" is not a fixed destination, but a journey we take together, hand in hand, through all the twists and turns.

The Art of Conflict: Communication and Resolution

Decoding the Dance of Disagreement: Your Guide to Conflict Styles

Let's face it, conflict is as much a part of being human as laughter or a good cup of coffee. It's the inevitable bump in the road of any relationship, whether it's with your partner, your boss, or even yourself. But while we often dread it, conflict isn't inherently bad. In fact, when handled well, it can be a powerful catalyst for growth, understanding, and stronger connections. The secret? Understanding the intricate dance of conflict styles and recognizing the triggers that set us off.

This isn't about turning you into a conflict ninja overnight. It's about giving you a practical toolkit for navigating disagreements with grace and confidence. We'll delve into the fascinating world of conflict styles, dissecting common patterns like avoidance, accommodation, and aggression, and exploring how they impact our relationships. Think of it as a backstage pass to the drama of human interaction. We'll also shine a light on those pesky triggers that ignite the flames of conflict, giving you the insights you need to recognize and manage them before things escalate.

The Conflict Style Carousel: Where Do You Ride?

We all have a unique way of approaching conflict, shaped by our personalities, upbringing, cultural background, and past experiences. These predispositions often manifest as distinct conflict styles – consistent patterns of behavior and communication during disagreements. While we rarely stick rigidly to one style, recognizing our dominant tendencies can provide valuable clues to our reactions in conflict situations. It's like recognizing your favorite dance move – you might try others, but you always come back to that familiar groove.

1. The Vanisher (Avoidance):

Imagine a turtle retreating into its shell. That's avoidance in a nutshell. People with this style tend to sidestep or withdraw from conflict, changing the subject, postponing discussions, or simply remaining silent. They often prioritize maintaining peace and avoiding confrontation, fearing potential damage to the relationship or experiencing discomfort with strong emotions.

The Ripple Effect: While avoidance might offer temporary relief, it can have detrimental long-term effects. Unresolved issues fester, creating resentment and distance. It can also communicate a lack of care or respect, leading to feelings of invalidation and frustration. Over time, avoidance can erode trust and intimacy, preventing genuine connection and problem-solving.

Real-World Scenario: Picture a couple struggling with debt. One partner consistently avoids discussing finances, even when the situation becomes dire. This avoidance might temporarily ease anxiety, but it prevents them from addressing the root cause and working together towards a solution. Eventually, the unresolved financial stress can lead to arguments, mistrust, and even relationship breakdown.

Workplace Drama: A team is tasked with implementing new software. Several members have concerns about usability and workload, but avoid voicing them to the project manager, fearing they'll be seen as negative. The project proceeds without addressing these critical issues, leading to significant problems during implementation, including delays, errors, and plummeting team morale.

2. The Pleaser (Accommodation):

This style is all about yielding to the other party's wishes, often at the expense of one's own needs. Individuals with this tendency prioritize harmony, even if it means sacrificing their own interests. They're often highly cooperative and agreeable, putting others' needs ahead of their own.

The Price of Peace: While accommodation can foster short-term peace, it can breed resentment and dissatisfaction over time. Consistently neglecting your own needs can lead to feelings of being taken advantage of, unheard, or undervalued. It can create an imbalance of power in the relationship, where one party constantly gives in while the other benefits.

Dinner Dilemma: A group of friends is deciding on a restaurant. One person desperately wants to try a new Ethiopian place, but the others prefer Italian. To avoid conflict, the Ethiopian enthusiast agrees to Italian, even though they're disappointed. While seemingly a small concession, consistently accommodating others can lead to resentment and a sense of not being heard.

Vacation Veto: A married couple plans their annual vacation. One spouse dreams of a relaxing beach getaway, while the other craves an adventurous hiking trip. To avoid an argument, the beach-lover agrees to the hiking trip, despite not being physically fit and disliking strenuous activity. This leads to a miserable vacation for both, one exhausted and the other riddled with guilt.

3. The Crusader (Aggression):

This style involves forcefully asserting one's needs, often at the expense of others. Individuals might be verbally abusive, intimidating, or even physically aggressive. They might interrupt, dominate conversations, and use blaming or accusatory language, focusing on winning the argument and controlling the outcome.

The Fallout: Aggression creates a hostile and unsafe environment, damaging trust and intimacy. It can lead to fear, resentment, and a breakdown in communication. While it might achieve short-term compliance, it ultimately undermines relationships and creates lasting negative consequences.

Manager Meltdown: A manager berates an employee in front of colleagues for a minor mistake, using harsh language and belittling comments. While seemingly asserting authority, this damages the employee's morale, reduces productivity, and creates a climate of fear.

Sibling Showdown: Two siblings argue over a shared computer. One resorts to yelling, name-calling, and physically pushing the other away. This aggressive behavior creates fear and resentment, damaging their relationship and hindering conflict resolution.

Turning Down the Heat: Taming the Flames of Conflict

Let's face it, conflict is as much a part of being human as laughter or a craving for pizza. It's messy, uncomfortable, and sometimes feels like a runaway train. But just like a skilled conductor can bring a speeding train to a safe stop, we can learn to de-escalate conflict and steer it towards a more productive destination. This isn't about pretending disagreements don't exist; it's about transforming them from destructive fires into controlled burns that clear the way for growth.

Think of conflict like a simmering pot. Left unattended, it boils over, creating a mess and potentially causing serious damage. Our job is to tend the pot, to understand the heat source, and to know when to turn down the flame.

From Sparks to Inferno: Understanding the Escalation Ladder

Imagine a conflict as climbing a ladder. At the bottom, it's a minor disagreement, a slight difference of opinion. But each rung you climb takes you further from resolution and closer to a full-blown conflagration. Friedrich Glasl's Nine-Stage Model is like a map of this treacherous climb, showing us how things can spiral out of control:

Hardening: We dig in our heels, convinced we're right. The other person becomes "the enemy."
Debates and Polemics: Logic flies out the window. It's not about understanding anymore; it's about winning.
Actions not Words: We stop talking and start acting out our frustrations. Think silent treatment or passive-aggressive behavior.
Images and Coalitions: We paint the other person as a monster and rally our "troops" for support.
Loss of Face: Public humiliation becomes the weapon of choice.
Strategies of Threats: Ultimatums and veiled threats enter the picture.
Limited Destructive Blows: We start inflicting targeted damage, whether emotional or otherwise.
Fragmentation of the Enemy: The goal is no longer just to win, but to obliterate the other side.

Together into the Abyss: We're willing to go down with the ship, as long as the other person suffers too.

Knowing these stages is like having a weather forecast for a storm. It helps us anticipate what might happen and prepare accordingly.

Cooling Down the Combustion: Practical De-escalation Tools

So, how do we turn down the heat and climb back down that ladder? Here are some essential tools:

Self-Soothing First: You can't pour from an empty cup. If you're feeling emotionally charged, take a break. Deep breaths, a walk around the block, or even just closing your eyes for a moment can work wonders. Think of it as putting on your own oxygen mask before assisting others.

Listen Up (Really Listen): Active listening isn't just about hearing words; it's about understanding the emotions behind them. Put down your phone, make eye contact, and resist the urge to interrupt. Reflect back what you're hearing to ensure you're on the same page. "So, if I understand correctly, you're feeling frustrated because...?"

Empathy: Walking a Mile in Their Shoes: Try to see the situation from the other person's perspective, even if you don't agree with it. Acknowledge their feelings. "I can see why you're upset. That sounds really difficult." This doesn't mean you're condoning their behavior; it just shows you're listening and respecting their experience.

Space: The Final Frontier: Sometimes, the best thing you can do is create some distance. Suggest a cooling-off period. "I think we both need a few minutes to cool down. Let's take a break and come back to this later."

Focus on the Problem, Not the Person: Avoid personal attacks. Stick to the issue at hand. Instead of "You're always so inconsiderate," try "I felt hurt when..."

"I" Statements: Your Secret Weapon: Express your own feelings and needs without blaming the other person. "I feel frustrated when..." is much less confrontational than "You make me angry."

Curiosity: The Power of Questions: Ask open-ended questions to understand the other person's perspective. "Can you tell me more about what happened?" This shows you're genuinely interested in their point of view.

Finding Common Ground: The Bridge to Resolution: Even in the most heated conflicts, there's usually some common ground. Find it. Maybe you both want what's best for your children, or maybe you both want the project to succeed. Focusing on shared goals can create a foundation for finding solutions.

The Evolving Landscape of Conflict Resolution

Just like technology, our understanding of conflict resolution is constantly evolving. We're learning more about the impact of trauma, the importance of cultural sensitivity, and the role of technology in online disputes. AI tools are even being developed to help us analyze communication patterns and identify potential triggers.

The Takeaway:

De-escalating conflict is a skill, not an innate talent. It takes practice, patience, and a willingness to understand the other person's perspective. But the rewards are immense: stronger relationships, more productive workplaces, and a more peaceful world. So, the next time you feel the heat rising, remember these tools and turn down the flame. You might be surprised at the positive change you can create.

Navigating the Human Connection: Expressing Needs, Setting Boundaries, and Resolving Disagreements

Let's face it, communication isn't always sunshine and rainbows. It's messy, nuanced, and sometimes downright frustrating. But it's also the lifeblood of our relationships, both at home and at work. Think of it like this: good communication is the bridge that connects us, while poor communication is the chasm that divides us. This exploration dives into the art of constructive communication, offering practical strategies to express your needs, establish healthy boundaries, and navigate disagreements with grace and effectiveness.

Speaking Your Truth: Expressing Needs Effectively

Expressing your needs isn't about being demanding; it's about being human. It's about recognizing that your needs matter and learning how to articulate them in a way that resonates with others. Think of it as planting seeds: you need to carefully choose the right time and place, nurture them with the right words, and tend to them with active listening.

Know Thyself: Before you can express your needs, you need to understand them. Take some time for introspection. What truly matters to you? What are your non-negotiables? What are you willing to compromise on? The clearer you are about your own needs, the more confidently and effectively you can communicate them.

Instead of a vague feeling of "unease" at work, pinpoint specific needs like "regular check-ins with my manager" or "opportunities to present my work."

Timing is Everything: Imagine trying to have a serious conversation during a chaotic family dinner or a stressful deadline at work. Not ideal, right? Choose a time when you and the other person are calm, focused, and have the space for a meaningful exchange. A quiet coffee date or a scheduled one-on-one meeting can make all the difference.

The Power of "I": "You" statements can feel accusatory and put people on the defensive. "I" statements, on the other hand, focus on your experience and feelings. They're a way of expressing your truth without blaming the other person. For example, instead of saying, "You always interrupt me," try, "I feel unheard and frustrated when I'm interrupted." It's a subtle shift, but it can dramatically change the dynamic of the conversation.

Paint a Clear Picture: Vagueness breeds confusion. Be specific and concrete when expressing your needs. Instead of saying, "I need more help," try, "I could really use help with the kids' bedtime routine on weeknights." The more detail you provide, the better the chances of your needs being understood and met.

Listen Up! Communication is a two-way street. Expressing your needs is only half the battle. The other half is actively listening to the other person's response. Pay attention not just to their words, but also to their body language and tone. Show genuine interest in their perspective, even if you don't agree with it.

Collaboration, Not Confrontation: Expressing needs isn't about making demands; it's about opening a dialogue.

Be prepared to brainstorm solutions together and find common ground. Compromise isn't about losing; it's about creating a win-win situation.

Protecting Your Peace: Setting Healthy Boundaries

Boundaries are the invisible lines that define what you're comfortable with. They're essential for self-care and maintaining healthy relationships. Think of them as the guardrails that keep you on track and prevent you from veering off into burnout or resentment.

Know Your Limits: What drains your energy? What makes you feel uncomfortable or disrespected? Reflect on your past experiences to identify your boundaries. Are you constantly saying "yes" when you really mean "no"? Do you feel pressured to take on more than you can handle? Understanding your limits is the first step to setting effective boundaries.

Direct and Kind: When communicating your boundaries, be clear, direct, and respectful. Avoid hinting or being passive-aggressive. A simple, "I'm not available to take on any more projects right now" is often sufficient.

Consistency is Key: Setting boundaries is like training a muscle: it takes practice and consistency. People might test your boundaries initially, so it's important to stand your ground. The more consistent you are, the more likely people are to respect your boundaries.

The Art of "No": "No" is a complete sentence. You don't need to over-explain or make excuses. A simple, "No, thank you," is perfectly acceptable. If you feel it's appropriate, you can offer an alternative or suggest a different time.

Respect the Boundaries of Others: Just as you expect others to respect your boundaries, you need to respect theirs. Pay attention to their verbal and nonverbal cues. If someone says they're not comfortable with something, respect their wishes.

Turning Conflict into Connection: Resolving Disagreements Constructively

Disagreements are inevitable. But how you handle them can make or break a relationship. Think of disagreements as opportunities for growth and deeper understanding.

Stay Cool, Calm, and Collected: When conflict arises, take a deep breath and resist the urge to react impulsively. Staying calm and respectful is crucial for productive communication.

Focus on the Issue, Not the Person: Avoid personal attacks or name-calling. Stick to the facts and address the specific issue at hand.

Listen with Your Whole Heart: Truly listen to the other person's perspective. Try to understand where they're coming from, even if you don't agree with them.

Find Common Ground: Even in the midst of a disagreement, there are often areas of common ground. Identify these areas and build on them.

Brainstorm Together: Approach conflict as a team, working together to find solutions that work for everyone involved.

Know When to Step Away: If the discussion becomes too heated, it's okay to take a break. Cool down and come back to the conversation later when you're both feeling more rational.

Communication is a lifelong journey, not a destination. By practicing these skills, you can build stronger, more meaningful relationships and navigate the complexities of human interaction with greater ease and confidence.

The Whispers of the Heart: Forgiveness and Reconciliation

Forgiveness and reconciliation. These aren't just words; they're the delicate threads that weave through the tapestry of human relationships, especially when that fabric has been torn by hurt and betrayal. They represent the profound capacity we have to heal, not just ourselves, but the connections we cherish. Imagine them as twin flames, flickering with the potential for warmth and light, even in the darkest of times. This isn't about simply saying "I forgive you" or pretending nothing happened. It's a journey, a complex dance of emotions, thoughts, and actions that requires courage, vulnerability, and a deep understanding of the human heart.

Forgiveness: Untangling the Knots Within

Forgiveness is often painted as a gift we give to the person who hurt us. But what if we reframed it? What if, instead, it's a gift we give ourselves? It's not about condoning the wrong that was done, or even forgetting it. It's about releasing ourselves from the heavy chains of resentment, anger, and the burning desire for revenge. Think of it like carrying a heavy stone. Forgiveness is setting that stone down, freeing your hands and your heart to move forward.

The path to forgiveness isn't a straight line; it's more like a winding trail with its own unique twists and turns. We might stumble, we might even backtrack, but eventually, we can find our way to a place of peace. One model describes this journey in stages:

The Unveiling: This is where we acknowledge the pain, the raw, unfiltered emotions that come with being hurt. We allow ourselves to feel the sting of betrayal, the ache of disappointment. Suppressing these feelings only delays the healing process.

The Crossroads: This is the moment of decision. Do we choose to cling to our anger, letting it fester and consume us? Or do we choose the path of forgiveness, knowing it won't be easy, but that it ultimately leads to freedom?

The Climb: This is the active work of forgiveness. It might involve trying to understand the other person's perspective, not to excuse their actions, but to perhaps understand the context. It might involve grappling with our own role in the situation. This stage can be incredibly challenging, and sometimes, we need a guide, like a therapist, to help us navigate the difficult terrain.

The Summit: This is where we find a sense of peace, not necessarily forgetting what happened, but no longer defined by it. The emotional charge of the hurt diminishes, and we can move forward with a sense of closure.

What Helps Us Forgive?

Forgiveness isn't something we can force. It's nurtured by certain conditions:

Walking in Their Shoes: Empathy, the ability to see the world from another's perspective, can be a powerful catalyst. It doesn't mean condoning their actions, but understanding them as another flawed human being.

A Bridge of Words: A sincere apology can be incredibly healing. When someone acknowledges their wrongdoing and expresses genuine remorse, it validates our pain and opens the door to forgiveness.

The Ties That Bind: Our relationship with the person who hurt us matters. Forgiveness is often more likely when we have a close bond with the offender, like a family member or a dear friend.

Inner Compass: Our personal values and beliefs play a significant role. If we value compassion, understanding, and personal growth, we may be more inclined to choose forgiveness as a path to healing.

The Healer Time: Forgiveness takes time. It's not a race. We need to allow ourselves the space and grace to process our emotions at our own pace.

A Guiding Hand: Therapy can be invaluable, especially when dealing with deep-seated hurt or trauma. A therapist can provide a safe space to explore our emotions and develop healthy coping mechanisms.

Reconciliation: Mending the Broken Pieces

While forgiveness is an internal process, reconciliation is about rebuilding a relationship. It's a joint effort, a dance between two (or more) people who are willing to work together to heal the rift between them. It's not always possible, or even healthy, especially in situations involving abuse or repeated harm. But when both parties are committed, reconciliation can create a stronger, more resilient bond.

The Ingredients for Reconciliation:

Forgiveness, Shared: Reconciliation can't happen if either party is still harboring resentment. Both individuals need to engage in their own process of forgiveness.

Speaking from the Heart: Open and honest communication is paramount. Both parties need to be willing to express their feelings, listen to each other without judgment, and acknowledge their part in the conflict.

Stepping into Each Other's World: Empathy is crucial. Trying to understand each other's experiences and perspectives, even if we don't agree with them, can build bridges of understanding.

A Pledge to Change: Reconciliation requires a commitment to change. This might involve learning better communication skills, setting healthy boundaries, and developing more constructive ways of dealing with conflict.

Common Ground: Shared values and goals can provide a solid foundation for rebuilding. They remind us of what we have in common and what we're working towards.

The Slow Build of Trust: Trust is often shattered in the wake of betrayal. Rebuilding it takes time, consistency, and a genuine commitment to honesty and integrity.

Stories of Healing:

The Brothers' Reunion: John and Mark, estranged for years after a bitter argument, found their way back to each other after John's health scare. It wasn't easy, but through heartfelt conversations and a willingness to forgive, they rebuilt their bond, stronger and more meaningful than before.

A Love Reborn: Sarah and David, shattered by infidelity, chose to fight for their marriage. Through therapy and a commitment to honesty and change, they not only healed their relationship but discovered a deeper level of intimacy and understanding.

The Journey Continues:
Forgiveness and reconciliation are not one-time events; they're ongoing journeys. There will be bumps along the

road, moments of doubt and pain. But with patience, compassion, and a willingness to keep moving forward, we can find healing, growth, and a deeper appreciation for the power of human connection.

Trust and Intimacy in the Digital Age

The Tightrope Walk of Love: Why Vulnerability is Both Terrifying and Essential

We all crave deep, meaningful connections. We long to be seen, understood, and accepted for who we truly are, quirks, flaws, and all. But the path to intimacy is paved with vulnerability, a tightrope walk between the exhilarating heights of connection and the dizzying drop of potential heartbreak. It's a paradox, really: the very thing that can bring us the greatest joy is also the thing that scares us the most. This tightrope, this vulnerability paradox, is the central drama of our love lives.

Think about it. Vulnerability isn't just spilling your deepest secrets (though that can be part of it). It's the quiet courage to be yourself, even when you're not sure you'll be accepted. It's admitting you're scared, or that you need help, or that you just really, really care. It's showing up authentically, without the masks we often wear to protect ourselves. Brené Brown, that vulnerability guru, nailed it when she called it "uncertainty, risk, and emotional exposure." It's the birthplace of courage, connection, and all the good stuff, but man, is it terrifying.

Why so scary? Because when we drop our guard, we become... well, vulnerable. We expose our soft underbelly to the world, and that's a risky business. We fear rejection, that someone will see our true selves and decide we're not good enough, not worthy of love. We worry about betrayal, that our trust will be broken, leaving us feeling foolish and hurt. We might even fear simply being misunderstood, that our vulnerability will be met with a blank stare or worse, indifference, making us feel small and insignificant.

These fears can lead us to build walls around our hearts, creating a safe but lonely fortress. We might engage in surface-level relationships, keeping everyone at arm's length to avoid the possibility of pain. It's like living in a bubble – safe, maybe, but also cut off from the richness and vibrancy of true connection.

But here's the kicker: while vulnerability is risky, it's also the key to everything we crave in relationships. It's the secret ingredient to deep intimacy, the kind that makes you feel truly seen and understood. It's how we build trust, that essential foundation for any meaningful bond. When someone shows us their vulnerability, it signals trust, inviting us to reciprocate and creating a beautiful cycle of openness.

Vulnerability also fuels emotional connection. Sharing our feelings and experiences allows others to truly empathize with us, creating a sense of shared humanity and understanding. It's like saying, "Hey, I'm human, just like you," and finding comfort in that shared experience. And let's be honest, relationships where people are genuinely vulnerable are just... better. They're more fulfilling, more satisfying, and more likely to last. Plus, embracing vulnerability can be incredibly empowering. Facing our fears and insecurities head-on can build resilience and self-awareness, helping us grow into stronger, more authentic versions of ourselves.

So, how do we navigate this tricky terrain? It's not about being vulnerable with everyone, all the time. That's a recipe for disaster. It's about being discerning, choosing carefully who we trust with our deeper selves. It's about starting small, sharing little bits of ourselves and seeing how they're received. It's about setting healthy boundaries, knowing what we're comfortable sharing and what we're not. And it's definitely about being kind to ourselves, especially when we take a risk and it doesn't go as planned.

Think of Sarah, who, after a painful divorce, was terrified to open up in her new relationship. Her new partner, Mark, understood her hesitancy and patiently showed her he was trustworthy. He listened without judgment, validated her feelings, and even shared his own vulnerabilities. Slowly, Sarah began to let him in, and their connection deepened into something truly special.

Or consider David, who thought showing emotions was a sign of weakness. His partner, Emily, gently encouraged him to open up, assuring him of her support. Through therapy, he learned to identify and express his feelings, strengthening not only his relationship with Emily but also his own sense of well-being.

These stories remind us that vulnerability is not weakness; it's courage. It's the courage to be ourselves, the courage to connect, the courage to love, even knowing that we might get hurt. It's a risk, yes, but it's a risk worth taking. Because on the other side of vulnerability lies the possibility of true, deep, and lasting love. And isn't that what we all long for?

Love in the Time of Algorithms: Navigating the Heart in a Digital World

Forget the quill and parchment – Cupid's arrow now flies through fiber optic cables. The digital revolution has not just changed how we communicate, it's fundamentally reshaped what intimacy even means. We're no longer just whispering sweet nothings; we're broadcasting snippets of our lives to curated audiences, blurring the lines between public and private, and redefining connection in the process. So, how do we navigate this new terrain of the heart, where love can blossom in a DM and wither under the harsh glare of a poorly filtered selfie?

Intimacy: It's Not Just Netflix and Chill Anymore (But That Helps):

Intimacy, that beautiful, messy, vulnerable dance of shared selves, has always been a tricky thing to define. Now, throw in algorithms, emojis, and the constant hum of notifications, and it gets even more complex. It's not just about sharing secrets whispered in the dark; it's about tagging each other in memes that perfectly encapsulate your shared sense of the absurd. It's about leaving a heart emoji on a post about their cat, even though you're secretly allergic. It's about the curated highlight reel of your life meeting the messy, unfiltered reality behind the scenes.

Social Media: The Ultimate Wingman (and Saboteur):

Social media is like that friend who means well but occasionally sets your hair on fire. It can connect you with like-minded souls across continents, offer a platform for vulnerable expression, and even help you find your tribe. Think of the support groups that blossom in the digital space, offering solace and connection to those facing similar challenges. But then there's the highlight reel effect, the constant barrage of perfectly posed lives that can leave you feeling like your own relationship is a crumpled-up napkin compared to a masterpiece. And don't even get me started on the dreaded "seen" notification... talk about pressure.

Case Study: The Emoji and the Heartbreak:

Imagine a study (because we love studies!) that explores the correlation between Instagram filters and relationship satisfaction. Researchers might find that couples who spend more time crafting the perfect aesthetic for their online presence spend less time actually connecting in the real world. The study could also reveal a link between excessive scrolling and feelings of inadequacy, as couples compare their perfectly imperfect lives to the seemingly flawless portrayals of others. The key takeaway? Sometimes, the best filter is no filter at all.

Online Dating: Swiping Right on a Brave New World:

Online dating has democratized the search for love, offering a smorgasbord of potential partners at our fingertips. It's like a cosmic dating buffet, where you can sample different flavors until you find something that tantalizes your taste buds. But the sheer volume of choice can be overwhelming, leading to "choice paralysis" and a fear of missing out on someone just a little bit better. And let's be honest, sometimes the carefully crafted profile is more fiction than fact.

Virtual Communication: Bridging the Distance (and Creating New Ones):

Video calls, instant messaging, and shared playlists – these are the digital threads that keep long-distance relationships alive. They allow us to share moments, even when miles apart, creating a sense of shared presence. But the nuances of human interaction can get lost in translation. A misinterpreted text can lead to a full-blown argument, and the lack of physical touch can leave a lingering ache.

Case Study: Love in the Time of Lag:

Picture a study that delves into the challenges and triumphs of long-distance couples who rely heavily on virtual communication. Researchers could discover that couples who schedule regular "digital dates," engage in shared online activities (like watching movies together), and communicate openly about their needs and expectations are more likely to maintain intimacy and relationship satisfaction.

The Future of Digital Intimacy: Ready Player Love?

Virtual reality, augmented reality, and the metaverse – these are the next frontiers of digital intimacy. Imagine holding hands with your partner in a virtual café, even if you're thousands of miles apart. Or using AR to leave digital love notes scattered around your city for your partner to discover. The possibilities are both exciting and a little bit terrifying.

The Bottom Line: Humanity, Ctrl+Alt+Deleted?

Technology is a tool, and like any tool, it can be used for good or ill. It can amplify our connections, deepen our intimacy, and bring us closer to the people we love. But it can also create distance, foster unrealistic expectations, and leave us feeling more alone than ever. The key is to be mindful, to set boundaries, and to remember that true intimacy is about more than just likes and followers. It's about the messy, beautiful, vulnerable reality of human connection, both online and off. So, put down your phone for a minute, look into the eyes of someone you love, and remember what it feels like to connect heart to heart, not just screen to screen.

The Long, Winding Road Back to Us: Healing After Betrayal

Imagine trust as a beautifully woven tapestry, each thread representing a promise, a shared secret, a feeling of safety. Betrayal, like a jagged tear, rips through this fabric, leaving behind a gaping hole and frayed edges. Rebuilding isn't about simply patching it up; it's about painstakingly re-weaving, thread by thread, creating something even stronger and more resilient than before. It's a journey fraught with pain, vulnerability, and the constant question: can we ever truly trust again?

This isn't a journey for the faint of heart. It's a climb up a steep mountain, often slippery and treacherous. There will be moments of doubt, of wanting to turn back, of questioning whether the summit – a place of renewed trust and connection – is even reachable. But with courage, honesty, and a deep commitment to healing, it is possible to find your way back to each other, even stronger than before.

The Earthquake Within: Understanding the Devastation

Betrayal isn't just an event; it's an earthquake that shakes the very foundations of a relationship. It shatters the bedrock of safety and predictability, leaving behind a landscape of emotional rubble. For the betrayed partner, the world can suddenly feel like it's tilting on its axis. Waves of shock, anger, grief, and a profound sense of violation can crash over them, leaving them feeling lost and adrift. Sleep becomes a battlefield, appetite vanishes, and the simplest things can trigger a cascade of painful memories. The voice inside whispers, "How could you do this to me?"

The betrayer, too, is often caught in a maelstrom of emotions. Guilt, shame, and remorse can be overwhelming, but so can defensiveness and denial. It's tempting to minimize the damage, to rationalize the actions, but true healing requires facing the truth, however painful it may be. It means asking the difficult questions: "Why did I do this?" "What needs to change within me?"

The Architect of Trust: Building Back Better

Rebuilding trust is an active, collaborative process. It's not something that just happens; it requires both partners to roll up their sleeves and get to work. Here are some of the essential tools in the trust-builder's toolkit:

Radical Honesty: No more secrets, no more half-truths. The betrayer must be willing to answer the difficult questions, to shine a light into the darkest corners, even when it's uncomfortable. Transparency is the oxygen of trust.

Empathy in Action: Saying "I'm sorry" is just the beginning. The betrayer must demonstrate a deep understanding of the pain they've inflicted. It's about listening without defensiveness, acknowledging the hurt, and validating the betrayed partner's feelings.

Actions Speak Louder: Trust isn't built on words; it's built on consistent, reliable actions. The betrayer must demonstrate their commitment to change in every aspect of the relationship. It's about showing, not just telling.

Professional Guidance: A therapist can be an invaluable guide on this difficult journey. They can provide a safe space for both partners to process their emotions, understand the dynamics of the betrayal, and learn healthier ways of communicating.

Time: The Great Healer (and Tester): There are no shortcuts to rebuilding trust. It takes time, patience, and a willingness to ride the emotional rollercoaster. There will be good days and bad days, but consistency and commitment are key.

A Shared Vision: Rebuilding trust isn't just about going back to the way things were. It's about creating a new "us," a relationship built on a foundation of honesty, respect, and mutual understanding.

Navigating the Terrain: Stages of Healing

The journey of trust repair often unfolds in stages:

The Fallout: The initial shock, the raw emotions, the disorientation.

Truth and Reconciliation: The painful process of disclosure and understanding.

Rebuilding and Repair: The slow, deliberate work of rebuilding trust through consistent actions.

Forgiveness (A Personal Choice): A journey in itself, not a requirement for rebuilding trust.

Growth and Renewal: The emergence of a stronger, more resilient relationship.

Stories of Resilience: Finding Hope in the Darkness

Every story of betrayal and healing is unique. There's no one-size-fits-all approach. But what these stories share is a common thread: the courage to face the pain, the willingness to be vulnerable, and the unwavering belief that healing is possible. These stories remind us that even after the most devastating betrayals, love and trust can be rebuilt, stronger and more profound than before.

The Road Ahead: Embracing the Journey

Rebuilding trust is not easy. It's a long and winding road, filled with potholes and detours. But it's also a road that can lead to profound growth, both individually and as a couple. If you're willing to embark on this journey with honesty, vulnerability, and a deep commitment to healing, you can emerge on the other side with a relationship that is stronger, more resilient, and more deeply connected than you ever thought possible.

Let's talk about the digital age and how it's turned our ideas of privacy, boundaries, and even relationships upside down. It's like we're all living in a giant fishbowl, only it's made of data, and everyone's got a front-row seat.

Privacy: Remember when that meant a locked door? Now, it's more like trying to hold sand in your hand. Every click, every like, every online purchase leaves a trail. We're not just talking about names and addresses anymore; it's everything from our late-night browsing history (guilty!) to where we were last Tuesday. It's like our digital shadow is growing bigger and more detailed every day, and who knows who's looking at it?

This data collection thing gets creepy fast. Companies, governments, even that random person on the other side of the world – they might have access to bits and pieces of our lives. Think about the potential for identity theft, targeted ads that know you better than your best friend, or algorithms that decide your fate based on your online behavior. It's a brave new world, and not always in a good way.

And what about privacy in our actual relationships? The lines are so blurry now. What's okay to share online? A funny picture of your friend? A rant about your boss? Suddenly, the things we used to whisper to each other are broadcast to the world, and someone's feelings are bound to get hurt. Remember the Ashley Madison hack? Talk about a privacy nightmare. Lives were shattered, relationships destroyed, all because of a data breach. It's a stark reminder that what we put online can have real-world consequences.

Online Behavior: Where did "common sense" go? It feels like the rules of engagement have changed, and not for the better. People say things online they'd never say to someone's face. Cyberbullying runs rampant, hiding behind anonymity. Stalking and harassment have found a new playground. And don't even get me started on "revenge porn." It's a digital violation of the worst kind, and it's happening far too often.

Social media? It's a double-edged sword. It connects us, sure, but it also fuels envy, insecurity, and a constant pressure to project a perfect image. We're all curating our online selves, creating these highlight reels of our lives, and it's easy to get lost in the comparison game. The Gamergate controversy showed us just how toxic online interactions can become, with real-life repercussions for the people involved.

Self-Disclosure: How much is too much? Sharing personal stuff is how we build connections, but online, it's a whole different ballgame. We're all walking a tightrope between authenticity and oversharing. It's tempting to pour our hearts out online, but what happens when that information falls into the wrong hands? Trust is hard enough to build in person, but online, it's like trying to build a sandcastle in a hurricane. Catfishing, scams, fake profiles – it's a jungle out there. Online dating? Great way to meet people, but also a breeding ground for deception.

So, what do we do about it? Well, it's not going to be easy. We need to teach people how to navigate this digital world – digital literacy is key. We need to promote ethical online behavior – treat others the way you want to be treated, even behind a screen. Tech companies need to step up and strengthen privacy protections. And we need to have open conversations about all of this. Families, friends, communities – everyone needs to be part of the discussion.

The digital age is here to stay, and it's changing everything. We need to adapt, to learn, and to find a way to balance the benefits of technology with the fundamental human need for privacy, respect, and genuine connection. It's a wild ride, and we're all in it together.

The Language of Money: Financial Compatibility and Relationship Harmony

Talking Money: Let's Get Real About Finances

Money. It's something we all deal with, yet it can be one of the trickiest topics to navigate in any relationship, whether it's with your partner, family, or even close friends. It's not just about balancing the checkbook; it's about sharing your dreams, anxieties, and the baggage you might be carrying from past money experiences. Let's dive into why talking openly about finances is so crucial, how to actually do it without pulling your hair out, and what happens when we sweep money matters under the rug.

The Heart-to-Heart of Finances: Why Talking Money Matters for Happy Relationships

Think about it: how comfortable are you talking about money? For many, it's right up there with public speaking or discussing awkward medical issues. But research consistently shows a powerful link between open financial communication and happy, healthy relationships. When we can talk openly about money, it builds a bridge of trust, eases stress, and helps us row in the same direction. On the flip side, financial secrets and avoidance can breed resentment faster than you can say "budget shortfall."

Building a Money Love Connection: Sharing your financial hopes and fears is like showing someone a vulnerable part of yourself. It creates a deeper connection, a sense of "we're in this together." When you're honest about your income, debts, spending quirks, and big money goals, you're essentially saying, "I trust you with this important part of my life."

Stress Less, Share the Load: Money worries can be a huge weight on your shoulders. Talking about them with someone you trust is like sharing that load. You can brainstorm solutions together, offer each other support, and feel less alone in the financial wilderness.

Dreaming Big, Together: Financial discussions are golden opportunities to get on the same page about your dreams. Whether it's buying a house, traveling the world, or retiring early, talking about money allows you to align your goals and create a financial roadmap that reflects your shared vision.

Preventing Money Wars: Disagreements about money are a common relationship minefield. But by talking openly about spending habits, budgeting strategies, and priorities, you can identify potential trouble spots before they explode into full-blown arguments. It's like preventative maintenance for your relationship's finances.

Relationship Superglue: Couples who talk openly about money tend to have stronger, more resilient relationships. It makes sense, right? Open communication builds a foundation of trust, reduces stress, and fosters a sense of partnership – all key ingredients for a lasting bond.

Money Talk 101: Practical Tips for Productive Conversations

Okay, so talking about money is important. But how do you actually do it? Here are some tips to make those conversations less daunting and more productive:

Set the Mood: Don't try to have a serious financial discussion when you're exhausted, stressed, or surrounded by distractions. Choose a calm, comfortable time and place where you can both relax and focus.

Early and Often: Don't wait for a financial crisis to strike before talking about money. Start the conversation early in your relationship and make it a regular thing. Regular check-ins are like mini financial health assessments that can prevent bigger problems down the road.

Truth Serum Required: Honesty is non-negotiable. Be upfront about your income, debts, spending habits, and financial goals. Hiding anything, no matter how small, can erode trust and breed resentment.

Listen Up!: Financial communication isn't just about you talking; it's about truly listening to the other person. Pay attention, ask clarifying questions, and try to understand their perspective, even if you don't agree.

"I" Statements to the Rescue: When discussing sensitive money issues, "I" statements are your best friend. Instead of saying "You always overspend," try "I'm feeling a little worried about our budget because..." It's less accusatory and more likely to lead to a constructive conversation.

Solutions, Not Finger-Pointing: If disagreements pop up (and they probably will), focus on finding solutions together. Work as a team to create a plan that addresses both of your needs.

Patience is a Virtue: Changing financial habits and communication patterns takes time. Be patient with each other, celebrate small wins, and remember that this is a marathon, not a sprint.

When in Doubt, Call in the Pros: If you're really struggling to communicate effectively about finances, don't hesitate to seek help from a financial advisor or therapist. They can provide guidance and support to help you navigate these tricky conversations.

The Fallout: What Happens When Money Talks Go Silent

Financial secrecy and miscommunication can have serious consequences, from minor squabbles to major relationship breakdowns.

Trust Takes a Hit: Hiding financial information is a major trust breaker. Once that trust is damaged, it can be incredibly difficult to rebuild.

Resentment Brews: Unresolved financial issues can fester and create a toxic atmosphere in your relationship. Resentment can build up over time, poisoning the connection you share.

Financial Freefall: Secrecy and miscommunication can lead to poor financial decisions and instability. It's hard to budget, save, or manage debt effectively when you're not on the same page.

The Ultimate Price: In some cases, financial secrecy and miscommunication can lead to the end of the relationship. When trust is shattered and conflict becomes the norm, it can be hard to stay together.

Real-Life Lessons: Case Studies in Money Talk

The Spender and the Saver: A couple constantly clashed over money. One loved to spend, the other was a dedicated saver. Through therapy, they learned to talk openly about their financial values and create a budget that worked for both of them. The result? Fewer arguments and a stronger relationship.

The Secret Debt: A long-married couple faced a crisis when one partner discovered a mountain of hidden credit card debt. It was a huge blow to their trust. Through counseling, they addressed the underlying issues and created a plan to tackle the debt together. It was a tough journey, but it ultimately brought them closer.

The Bottom Line: Talking Money is Worth It

Open and honest communication about finances is the bedrock of healthy relationships. It builds trust, reduces stress, helps you achieve your dreams, and prevents conflict. It takes effort, but the rewards – a stronger, more fulfilling relationship – are definitely worth it. So, take a deep breath, grab a cup of coffee (or something stronger!), and start talking. Your relationship (and your wallet) will thank you.

Honey, We Need to Talk (About Money!): A Couple's Guide to Financial Harmony

Let's be honest, talking about money can be more awkward than running into your ex on a first date. But for couples, navigating shared finances is less about avoiding discomfort and more about building a solid foundation for your future together. Think of it as relationship "adulting" – not always glamorous, but definitely essential. This isn't just about balancing the checkbook (though that's important too!). It's about weaving your financial dreams together, like a cozy quilt of shared goals.

I. Budgeting: From "Uh Oh" to "Oh Yeah!":

A budget isn't a financial straitjacket; it's your personalized roadmap to "happily ever after" (or at least, "financially comfortable"). Think of it as a conversation, not a lecture.

A. Let's Get Down to Brass Tacks (and Bank Statements):

Financial Forensics: Time to play detective! Gather all your financial clues: pay stubs, bank statements, those tempting credit card offers (handle with care!), and any loan documents. Lay it all out on the table – transparency is key!

Income Inventory: Calculate your combined income – not just your regular paycheck, but also that side hustle you've been rocking, or any investment earnings. Every little bit counts!

Expense Expedition: Where does your money actually go? Track your spending for a month or two. You might be surprised to discover where those little expenses creep in (that daily latte adds up!). Use budgeting apps, spreadsheets, or even a cute notebook – whatever floats your boat.

Spending Safari: Now, analyze those spending habits. Are you spending more on "wants" than "needs"? No judgment here, but this is where you can identify areas to tweak.

Dream Weaving: What do you want to achieve together? A dream vacation? A cozy home? Early retirement? Define your short-term, mid-term, and long-term goals. The more specific, the better! (Think 'Trip to Bali in 2 years" instead of 'Travel more").

Money Mapping: Based on your income, expenses, and goals, allocate your funds. This is where you decide where each dollar goes – rent, groceries, savings, that new gadget you've both been eyeing...

Regular Check-ins: Life throws curveballs. Review your budget regularly (monthly or quarterly) and adjust as needed. A job change, a new furry family member, or even just a change in your coffee preferences can impact your finances.

B. Budgeting Styles: Find Your Groove:

50/30/20: A classic for a reason. 50% of your income for needs, 30% for wants, and 20% for savings and debt repayment. Simple and effective.

Zero-Based Budget: Every dollar has a purpose. Your income minus your expenses should equal zero. Great for meticulous planners.

Envelope System: A cash-based approach. Divide your budget into categories and put cash in envelopes. Once an envelope is empty, you're done spending in that category. A good way to curb impulse buys.

Digital Dynamos: Budgeting apps can be your best friend. They sync with your bank accounts, track expenses, and even help you set goals.

C. Budgeting in Action:

Let's say Sarah and David bring home $8,000 a month. Using the 50/30/20 rule:

Needs (50%): $4,000 (rent, utilities, groceries, transportation)
Wants (30%): $2,400 (dining out, hobbies, entertainment)
Savings & Debt Repayment (20%): $1,600 (emergency fund, down payment, student loans)

II. Saving: Building Your Financial Fortress:

Saving isn't just about putting money aside; it's about investing in your future.

A. Savings Goals: Big and Small:

Emergency Fund: Your financial superhero! Covers 3-6 months of living expenses in case of unexpected events.
Down Payment: Dreaming of a white picket fence? Start saving!
Retirement Nest Egg: Future you will thank you.
Education Fund: For your kids' future or your own lifelong learning.
Vacation Fund: Because you deserve a break!

B. Savings Strategies: Making it Happen:

Automate, Automate, Automate: Set up automatic transfers to your savings account. It's like magic!
Expense Trimming: Find those little leaks in your budget and plug them!

Income Boost: Explore ways to earn extra cash.

Employer Perks: Take advantage of retirement plans and matching contributions. It's free money!

Invest Wisely: Let your money work for you. Consult a financial advisor if needed.

C. Savings in Action:

Sarah and David want a $10,000 emergency fund. Saving $500 a month, they'll reach their goal in 20 months.

III. Joint Financial Decisions: Teamwork Makes the Dream Work:

Talking about money can be tough, but open communication is essential.

A. Communication is Key:

Regular Money Dates: Schedule time to discuss finances.

Transparency Time: Be honest about income, expenses, and debts.

Listen Up: Really hear each other's perspectives.

Respectful Dialogue: Even when things get tricky, keep it respectful.

B. Managing Money Together:

Joint Accounts: Combine everything into one account. Simple and transparent.

Separate Accounts: Maintain some financial independence.

Hybrid Approach: A mix of both!

C. Important Money Conversations:

   Debt Management: Create a plan to tackle debt.
   Investment Strategy: Discuss your risk tolerance and
goals.
   Big Purchases: Make joint decisions about major
expenses.
   Insurance Planning: Protect yourselves with adequate
coverage.
   Estate Planning: Plan for the future.

D. Example:

Sarah and David use a hybrid approach: separate
accounts for personal spending and a joint account for
shared expenses and savings.

IV. Navigating Financial Bumps in the Road:

Life happens. Be prepared for financial challenges.

A. Emergency Fund to the Rescue: Your financial cushion
for unexpected events.
B. Flexibility and Communication: Be willing to adjust your
plans.
C. Professional Guidance: Don't hesitate to seek help
from a financial advisor.

Managing finances as a couple is a journey, not a
destination. It's about working together, communicating
openly, and building a secure future, one dollar at a time.
So grab your partner, pour a glass of wine (or your favorite
beverage), and start talking! It might just be the most
important conversation you ever have.

Money Talks: More Than Just Numbers

Let's be honest, talking about money can be more awkward than discussing your weirdest childhood nickname. But ignoring it in a relationship is like ignoring a leaky faucet – eventually, it's going to flood the whole house. Financial disagreements aren't just about the dollars and cents; they're often about deeper stuff: values, dreams, and even a little bit of good old-fashioned fear. So, how do we navigate this tricky terrain without ending up in a financial free-for-all?

The Roots of the Money Mess:

Think of your financial philosophy as your money personality. Are you a "saver squirrel" diligently burying acorns for the future, or a "spendy sparrow" flitting from one exciting purchase to the next? These personalities can clash big time. Then you throw in things like power imbalances (one partner earning way more, or even just thinking they know more about money), unspoken expectations (like who pays for what, or whether you're saving for a house or a trip to Mars), and suddenly, you've got a recipe for a financial firestorm. And let's not forget the external pressures! Job loss, surprise expenses, or even just the general economic climate can turn up the heat on any relationship.

Taming the Financial Beast:

So, how do you move from financial foes to financial friends? Here's the secret sauce:

"Money Dates": No, not a romantic dinner with your bank statement. These are regular, dedicated times to chat about finances – goals, worries, the whole shebang. Think of it as a financial check-up for your relationship.

Listen Up (Really Listen): Put down your phone, make eye contact, and actually hear what your partner is saying. Try to understand their perspective, even if you don't agree with it. It's amazing how much tension melts away when you feel heard.

Compromise is Your BFF: Rarely is one person 100% right about money (unless you're Warren Buffett, in which case, teach me your ways!). Be prepared to bend a little, find middle ground, and create solutions that work for both of you.

Remember the "Why": Why are you together? Presumably, it's not just for the tax breaks. Focus on your shared dreams – that dream vacation, that cozy house, that secure future. These shared goals can be powerful motivators when you're bickering over budget lines.

No Name-Calling (Even of the Financial Kind): Avoid blaming or shaming your partner for their financial habits. Focus on the issue, not the person. You're a team, remember?

Get a Pro (Sometimes): If you're stuck in a financial rut, don't be afraid to call in the experts. A financial advisor can help you create a solid plan, and a therapist can help you navigate the emotional side of money.

Leveling the Playing Field:

Nobody wants to feel like they're being controlled by someone else's purse strings. Here's how to keep things balanced:

Transparency is Key: Share everything – income, debts, the whole financial picture. No secrets!

Two Heads are Better Than One: Involve both partners in big financial decisions, even if one earns more. Make sure everyone feels heard and valued.

Equal Access (Even with Separate Accounts): Even if you prefer separate bank accounts, make sure there's shared access to funds for joint expenses.

Financial Education for All: If one partner is a financial whiz and the other is still learning, share the knowledge! Empower each other to understand the world of finance.

Real-Life Relationship Roadblocks (and How to Navigate Them):

The Saver vs. The Spender: John and Mary learned to compromise by setting spending limits and focusing on shared goals like buying a house.

The Unequal Earners: Sarah and David tackled the power imbalance by openly communicating and creating a joint budget.

Financial Infidelity: The Ultimate Betrayal:

Hiding money or making secret financial decisions is a huge breach of trust. It requires honesty, transparency, and often, professional help to heal.

The Long Game: Planning for the Future:

Dream big! Talk about retirement, kids' education, and all those exciting life milestones. Create a long-term financial plan together and revisit it regularly.

The Bottom Line:

Talking about money might not be glamorous, but it's essential for a healthy relationship. By communicating openly, practicing empathy, and being willing to compromise, you can build a future of financial security and happiness together. Remember, you're on the same team, working towards the same goals. And sometimes, a little professional guidance can make all the difference.

The Whispers in the Wallet: Unmasking Financial Infidelity

Financial infidelity. The phrase itself feels cold, clinical. But the reality? It's a gut punch. A silent betrayal that chips away at the foundation of trust, leaving behind a wreckage of hurt and confusion. It's not just about the money; it's about the secrets, the lies, the erosion of shared dreams. It's a whisper in the wallet that can shatter a relationship.

We often think of infidelity in terms of stolen kisses or clandestine meetings. But financial infidelity is just as insidious. It's the secret Amazon purchases piling up in the closet, the gambling debts hidden beneath a veneer of normalcy, the quiet siphoning of funds into an account your partner doesn't know exists. It's the feeling of being blindsided, of realizing that the person you thought you knew, the person you trusted with your heart and your future, has been living a financial double life.

Imagine Sarah, discovering a mountain of credit card debt hidden by her husband, Mark. Not extravagant purchases, but a steady drip of seemingly small expenses that snowballed into a financial avalanche. The weight of the debt is crushing, but the real pain comes from the deception. The feeling that the man she loves has been lying to her face, treating her like a financial afterthought.

Or picture John, finding a separate bank account his wife, Lisa, has been quietly funding for years. Not for a rainy day, but for something – or someone – else. The money itself is secondary; it's the implication that stabs like a knife.

The unspoken message that she doesn't trust him, that she's building a separate life, a financial escape hatch.

Financial infidelity isn't always about huge sums. Sometimes, it's the small, consistent deceptions that sting the most. The inflated expense reports, the "forgotten" bills, the constant feeling that something isn't quite right. It's the drip, drip, drip of distrust that erodes the emotional landscape of the relationship.

It takes many forms. It can be the thrill of a secret online poker game, the comfort of a hidden shopping spree, or the calculated manipulation of shared resources. It can be a desperate attempt to regain control, a misguided effort to protect oneself, or a symptom of deeper relationship issues. Whatever the cause, the impact is undeniable. It's a breach of trust that can leave the betrayed partner feeling violated, foolish, and deeply insecure.

The road to recovery is long and arduous. It starts with brutal honesty, a complete and transparent accounting of all financial secrets. Then comes the difficult work of rebuilding trust, a process that requires vulnerability, empathy, and a willingness to confront the underlying issues that fueled the deception. Professional help, both financial and therapeutic, is often essential. It's about learning to communicate openly about money, setting healthy boundaries, and creating a shared vision for the future.

Sometimes, the damage is too deep. The whispers in the wallet become a roar, shattering the relationship beyond repair. But even in those cases, there can be a sense of closure, a chance to learn from the experience and build healthier relationships in the future.

Financial infidelity is a complex and painful issue, but it's one that needs to be talked about. It's time to break the silence, to shed the shame, and to recognize that financial betrayal is just as damaging as any other form of infidelity. It's time to listen to the whispers in the wallet, before they become a scream that tears everything apart.

Cultural Crossroads: Navigating Relationships Across Cultures

Culture, that invisible hand shaping our world, also molds the delicate architecture of our relationships. It whispers in our ears about what love should look like, how families should function, and even who we should choose to spend our lives with. These whispers, often unspoken, are what we call "cultural scripts"—the blueprints for our romantic and familial lives. Think of them as the unwritten rules of the relationship game, passed down through generations, influencing everything from how we flirt to how we raise our kids.

These scripts aren't etched in stone tablets, though. They're more like evolving stories, constantly being rewritten by societal shifts, technological leaps, and even the whispers of rebellion from those who dare to color outside the lines. We absorb these scripts from the moment we're born, watching our parents interact, listening to grandma's tales of courtship, and even from the rom-coms we binge-watch (guilty as charged!). They become so ingrained that we often don't even realize they're there, subtly guiding our expectations and behaviors.

Now, these scripts can be incredibly useful. They provide a sense of order, like a well-rehearsed play, making social interactions smoother and less anxiety-inducing. Imagine trying to navigate a first date without any idea of what's considered appropriate behavior – awkward, right? Scripts offer a shared understanding, reducing the risk of misinterpretations and hurt feelings. They also foster a sense of belonging, connecting us to our cultural roots and reinforcing shared values.

But here's the catch: these scripts aren't one-size-fits-all. Within any culture, you'll find variations, like different dialects of the same language. A family's socioeconomic status, their religious beliefs, where they live – all these things can tweak the script, leading to a beautiful tapestry of relationship styles. And, of course, individuals have agency! We're not just puppets following a pre-written plot. We can choose to improvise, to rewrite our own stories, blending tradition with personal preferences.

Take, for example, the concept of an "ideal relationship." In some cultures, the emphasis is on family ties and social stability, leading to arranged marriages where the union is as much about connecting families as it is about individual romance. I remember talking to a friend from India who, while initially hesitant about her arranged marriage, found deep love and respect for her husband over time. It challenged my own Western-centric view of romance, showing me that love can blossom in unexpected ways.

Contrast this with the Western ideal, often painted with broad strokes of romantic love, individual choice, and passionate connection. We're raised on stories of soulmates and "happily ever afters," where finding "the one" is the ultimate goal. But even within this framework, there's immense diversity. Dating in bustling New York City is a world away from dating in a small rural town.

Then there's courtship. In some cultures, it's a highly choreographed dance, with chaperones, strict rules, and limited interaction before marriage. In others, it's a free-flowing exploration, where individuals are encouraged to date multiple people before settling down. I remember my grandmother telling me stories of her courtship, where a stolen glance across the church aisle was considered a daring act! It's a stark contrast to the swipe-right culture of today.

Family dynamics also bear the imprint of cultural scripts. Some families operate like a well-oiled machine, with clear hierarchies and respect for elders. Others are more egalitarian, valuing individual autonomy and shared decision-making. In China, the concept of filial piety emphasizes the responsibility of children to care for their aging parents, a value that shapes family interactions and expectations.

And let's not forget mate selection. While love is often the driving force in Western societies, other cultures prioritize factors like social status, family background, or economic compatibility. Even in cultures where romance is paramount, cultural norms subtly influence who we find attractive and desirable.

The world is shrinking, thanks to globalization and migration, and our cultural scripts are evolving faster than ever. We're exposed to a kaleidoscope of relationship models, challenging traditional norms and creating beautiful hybrids. Intercultural relationships, once a rarity, are becoming increasingly common, bringing with them a unique set of challenges and rewards. Navigating different communication styles, family expectations, and cultural traditions can be tricky, but it can also be incredibly enriching, broadening our perspectives and deepening our understanding of love and commitment.

Technology, too, is a game-changer. Social media and dating apps have revolutionized how we meet and form relationships. They've democratized the dating process, allowing us to connect with people across the globe, but they've also introduced new complexities, like the pressure to present a perfect online persona and the blurring of lines between the digital and real worlds.

As we move forward, it's crucial to recognize the fluidity of cultural scripts and the agency of individuals in shaping their own relationships. There's no one "right" way to love or build a family. By embracing diversity and fostering open dialogue, we can create a world where all relationships, regardless of their cultural context, are celebrated and respected. The future of relationships is being written now, not on stone tablets, but in the ever-evolving stories we tell ourselves about love, commitment, and connection.

Weaving Worlds Together: Love, Language, and Laughter Across Cultures

Intercultural relationships – where hearts connect across continents and traditions intertwine – are like vibrant tapestries, rich with the colors of different backgrounds. Imagine two souls, each carrying the stories of their upbringing, their families, their very way of seeing the world, deciding to share their lives. It's an adventure, a dance of discovery, and yes, sometimes, a hilarious fumble with mispronounced words and misunderstood gestures. But beneath the surface, it's a powerful testament to love's ability to transcend boundaries.

Think about it: communication isn't just about words. It's a symphony of unspoken cues – the way we tilt our heads, the space we keep between us, even the rhythm of our laughter. Now, imagine trying to conduct that symphony with instruments tuned to different keys! That's the beautiful, messy reality of intercultural communication.

Lost in Translation? More Like Finding New Meaning!

Let's be real, sometimes it's going to feel like you're speaking different languages – even when you're both speaking English. One person might be used to getting straight to the point, while the other prefers a more roundabout approach, like telling a story with a moral woven in. It's like trying to assemble IKEA furniture with instructions in Klingon. Frustrating? Maybe. But also an opportunity to learn, to laugh, and to appreciate the beautiful diversity of human expression.

The Dance of "Yes" and "Maybe"

Ever been in a conversation where you weren't sure if "yes" meant "yes," "maybe," or "I'm just being polite"? Cultural context is everything! In some cultures, direct disagreement is considered rude, so people might use subtle cues to express their reservations. It's like reading between the lines of a Shakespearean sonnet – you need to be a detective of unspoken language.

Beyond Words: The Silent Language of Love

And then there's the silent language – the world of gestures, facial expressions, and personal space. A thumbs-up might be a sign of approval in one culture and an insult in another. Imagine the awkwardness! But these "oops" moments can also be incredibly endearing, reminding us that love is about more than just understanding each other's words; it's about understanding each other's hearts.

Tips for Harmony in the Cultural Symphony:

   Become a Super Listener: Listen not just to the words, but to the music behind them. Pay attention to your partner's body language, their tone, the things they don't say.
   Embrace the Awkward: Misunderstandings are inevitable. Don't be afraid to laugh at yourself (and with each other). It's all part of the adventure.

Become a Culture Detective: Learn about your partner's culture. Ask questions, explore their traditions, and try to see the world through their eyes.

Practice Empathy: Try to understand your partner's feelings, even if you don't agree with their perspective. Remember, love is about walking in each other's shoes (even if they're different sizes).

Be Patient, Grasshopper: Learning about another culture is a lifelong journey. Be patient with yourself, be patient with your partner, and enjoy the ride.

Find Your Funny Bone: Humor can be a lifesaver. Learn to laugh at the cultural mishaps (and there will be some!).

Say "I Love You" in Their Language: Even if it's just a few words, it shows you care. Plus, it's a fun way to learn a new language!

The Magic of Merging Worlds:

Intercultural relationships aren't always easy. There will be bumps in the road, moments of frustration, and times when you feel like you're on different planets. But the rewards are immeasurable. You'll learn to see the world in a new light, expand your understanding of love, and create a bond that is stronger and more beautiful because it has weathered the storms of cultural differences. It's like creating a new culture together, a unique blend of your two worlds. And that, my friends, is pure magic.

Bridging Worlds: Weaving Tapestries of Family

The world is shrinking, not in size, but in the distances between hearts. More and more, families are born from the beautiful collision of different cultures, creating vibrant tapestries woven with threads of diverse traditions, languages, and dreams. This isn't just about marriage anymore; it's about the intricate dance of integrating entire families, each with their own unique rhythm and history. It's a journey filled with both breathtaking vistas and unexpected detours, but ultimately, it's a testament to the enduring power of love to transcend boundaries.

Imagine a family reunion where the aroma of spicy kimchi mingles with the comforting scent of freshly baked apple pie. Picture grandparents telling stories in a language their grandchildren are only just beginning to understand, while laughter echoes across generations, a universal language understood by all. This is the magic of intercultural families – a symphony of shared experiences, a fusion of heritages, a living testament to the interconnectedness of our world.

But let's be real, it's not always rainbows and potlucks. Blending families from different backgrounds can be like trying to harmonize instruments that have never played together before. There will be dissonances, moments of misunderstanding, and the occasional clash of cymbals. Navigating these complexities requires more than just good intentions; it demands a willingness to listen deeply, to empathize genuinely, and to adapt gracefully.

Think about it: communication isn't just about words; it's about the unspoken language of gestures, the subtle nuances of tone, the cultural context that shapes our understanding. What's considered polite in one culture might be perceived as rude in another. Even something as simple as eye contact can carry vastly different meanings. Bridging these communication gaps requires patience, a genuine curiosity about the other's perspective, and a healthy dose of humility.

Then there are the cultural expectations, the invisible rules that govern family dynamics. One family might prioritize collective harmony, where individual needs are secondary to the well-being of the group. Another might champion individual expression and independence. Finding a balance between these often-conflicting values requires open dialogue, a willingness to compromise, and a shared commitment to building a family culture that honors both heritages.

And let's not forget the extended family, the aunts, uncles, and grandparents who bring their own unique perspectives and expectations to the mix. Navigating these intergenerational dynamics can be like walking a tightrope, balancing respect for tradition with the desire to create something new. It's about finding a way to honor the wisdom of the elders while also giving the younger generation the space to forge their own path.

The journey of intercultural family integration is a marathon, not a sprint. There will be moments of frustration, times when you feel like you're speaking different languages, even when you're speaking the same one. But amidst the challenges, there will also be moments of profound beauty, moments of connection that transcend cultural differences, moments when you realize that family is not defined by blood or origin, but by love, respect, and a shared commitment to building a life together.

In the years to come, as our world becomes increasingly interconnected, intercultural families will become even more common. They will be the norm, not the exception. And as they grow in number, they will continue to enrich our society, reminding us that diversity is not a weakness, but a strength. They will be the living embodiment of a world where bridges are built, not walls, and where love transcends all boundaries. They will be the future of family, a future that is as diverse and vibrant as the human spirit itself.

Weaving a Life Together: The Beautiful Complexity of Intercultural Love

Love knows no borders. In our increasingly interconnected world, intercultural relationships are blossoming, painting a vibrant picture of shared experiences and unique perspectives. But building a life together when you come from different cultural backgrounds is more than just romance; it's an adventure, a delicate dance of merging traditions, values, and worldviews to create something entirely new – a shared culture that honors both partners while forging a unique relationship identity. It's about crafting a "third culture," a beautiful blend that transcends the individual cultures and becomes something truly special.

More Than Just "Yours" and "Mine": The Dynamics of Cultural Integration

Cultural integration isn't about one partner simply adopting the other's culture. It's a vibrant, ongoing conversation, a negotiation, a compromise, and a creative act all rolled into one. It's about truly seeing and appreciating each other's cultural heritage, understanding the subtle language of different communication styles, and finding that sweet spot of shared values and beliefs. This journey can be challenging, absolutely, but it's also incredibly rewarding, opening up a world of understanding and building a relationship rich in diversity and resilience.

Think of it less like assimilation and more like jazz. Two distinct melodies come together, sometimes in harmony, sometimes in playful counterpoint, but always creating something beautiful and unique. It's not about erasing the individual notes, but about weaving them together into a richer, more complex song.

Blending Traditions: A Tapestry of Shared Experiences

One of the most visible and tangible ways intercultural couples create their shared culture is by blending traditions. This can be as grand as holiday celebrations or as intimate as daily routines.

Imagine the holidays: Do you celebrate Christmas and Hanukkah? Diwali and Thanksgiving? There's no single right answer. Many couples find joy in honoring both traditions, perhaps celebrating each separately, weaving elements together, or crafting entirely new traditions that become uniquely theirs. Maybe it's a fusion feast that combines family recipes from both sides, or a new holiday ritual that blends the best of both worlds. It's about creating memories that resonate with both of you.

Family dynamics can also be a fascinating landscape to navigate. Different expectations, communication styles, and family histories can present unique challenges. Open communication is key. It's about setting respectful boundaries, educating family members about each other's cultures, and gently guiding them to understand and appreciate your unique blend.

Even the everyday moments become opportunities for cultural integration. From the food you share to the language you speak at home, these small choices weave a rich tapestry of shared experience. Maybe you create a "house language" that's a mix of both your native tongues, or you find joy in exploring each other's culinary worlds, discovering new flavors and creating your own fusion dishes.

Building a Unique Identity: The "Third Culture"

Beyond blending existing traditions, intercultural couples have the incredible opportunity to create something entirely new: a "third culture." This shared identity isn't just a sum of its parts; it's a unique entity that emerges from your shared experiences, your laughter, your challenges, and your love.

It starts with identifying those core values that resonate with both of you. What truly matters? What are the non-negotiables? These deep conversations can be challenging, but they're essential for building a solid foundation.

Communication, of course, is crucial. Navigating different communication styles and language preferences requires patience, empathy, and a willingness to learn. Maybe you learn a few phrases in your partner's language, or you develop your own unique shorthand, a language of love that only you two understand.

And then there's the joy of creating new traditions, traditions that are entirely yours. Maybe it's a special anniversary ritual, a unique way of celebrating milestones, or a silly inside joke that becomes a cherished part of your story. These are the threads that weave your "third culture" together, creating a bond that's strong and uniquely yours.

Navigating the Ups and Downs: Challenges and Opportunities

Creating a shared culture isn't always smooth sailing. There will be bumps in the road. You might face prejudice, cultural misunderstandings, or conflicting expectations. But these challenges can also be incredible opportunities for growth and deeper understanding.

The key is to approach cultural differences with curiosity and respect, not judgment. Be willing to learn, to ask questions, and to see the world through your partner's eyes.

Remember, you're a team. Facing external pressures together can actually strengthen your bond. It's about presenting a united front and setting clear boundaries with family and friends.

Resilience is your superpower. Learn to communicate effectively, manage conflict constructively, and support each other through the inevitable ups and downs.

Real Love Stories: Inspiring Examples

Think of Aiko and David, who met in London and built a life together in the US. They learned to navigate different communication styles and family expectations, creating a beautiful blend of Japanese and American traditions. Or Priya and Marco, who bridged cultural gaps between India and Italy, creating a shared culture that celebrated both their heritages. These stories, and countless others, remind us that love truly can conquer all.

The Future of Intercultural Love

As our world becomes increasingly interconnected, intercultural relationships will continue to flourish. They challenge us to rethink our understanding of culture and identity, and they offer a beautiful glimpse into a more inclusive and understanding future. Intercultural couples, in their everyday lives, become ambassadors of cross-cultural understanding, enriching our world with their unique perspectives and their beautiful tapestry of shared experiences. Their stories remind us that love, in its most expansive form, has the power to connect us all.

Beyond Borders: The Complexities of Intercultural Relationships

Bridging the Silence: When Love Speaks a Different Language

In our increasingly interconnected world, love often blossoms across borders, weaving together tapestries of diverse cultures and backgrounds. These intercultural romances, vibrant and enriching, can paint our lives with breathtaking hues. Yet, sometimes, the most beautiful melodies are played with instruments tuned differently. Language, the very breath of communication, can become a stumbling block on the path to understanding, a silent wall between two hearts longing to connect. This isn't just about mispronounced words or grammatical hiccups; it's about the subtle dance of emotions lost in translation, the unspoken nuances that color our interactions.

Imagine trying to whisper a secret, a heartfelt confession, only to find the words crumbling on your tongue, lost in the labyrinth of unfamiliar sounds. Or picture the frustration of trying to explain a complex emotion, a swirling mix of joy and fear, only to have it reduced to a simplified, inadequate phrase. These aren't just inconveniences; they're tiny fractures in the foundation of intimacy, cracks that, if left unaddressed, can widen into chasms.

The impact of language barriers ripples through every facet of an intercultural relationship. It can make everyday tasks feel like Herculean labors. Ordering a simple meal can become a comedy of errors, asking for directions a frustrating game of charades. These daily struggles chip away at confidence and create a sense of dependence that can be deeply unsettling.

But the real challenge lies in the emotional realm. Language isn't just about conveying information; it's about sharing vulnerabilities, expressing affection, and building trust. When words fail, the heart can feel isolated, adrift in a sea of misunderstanding. The partner struggling with the language might feel like an outsider, peering into a world they can't fully access, while the more fluent partner might feel burdened by the constant need to translate, becoming a bridge instead of a fellow traveler.

And then there's the subtle power dynamic that can emerge. The partner who commands the dominant language might, unintentionally or otherwise, become the de facto decision-maker, their voice amplified, their perspective prioritized. This imbalance can breed resentment and create a sense of inequality within the relationship.

Yet, love, in its infinite wisdom, finds ways to transcend these obstacles. It whispers in the shared laughter, the gentle touch, the knowing glance. It builds bridges of understanding through shared experiences, mutual respect, and an unwavering commitment to connect.

So, how do we build those bridges?

Embrace the Adventure of Language Learning: Learning your partner's language isn't just about acquiring vocabulary; it's about opening a window into their soul, their culture, their very being. It's a tangible demonstration of love and commitment, a willingness to meet them on their own terms. And let's be honest, stumbling through a new language can be hilariously endearing!

Tech is Your Friend (But Use it Wisely): Translation apps and online dictionaries can be lifesavers, but they shouldn't become a crutch. They're tools to aid communication, not replace it. Don't let technology become a substitute for genuine human interaction.

Patience, My Dear, Patience: Communication is a two-way street, and it requires patience from both sides. Speak slowly, clearly, and avoid jargon. Listen actively, even when you're struggling to understand. Don't interrupt or finish your partner's sentences. Remember, vulnerability is a gift, and your partner is sharing a piece of themselves with you.

The Power of Nonverbal Cues: A smile, a hug, a hand squeeze – these are universal languages that transcend words. Pay attention to your partner's body language, their facial expressions, their tone of voice. Often, what's left unsaid speaks volumes. But be mindful that nonverbal cues can also be culturally nuanced. A gesture that's considered friendly in one culture might be offensive in another.

Celebrate the Differences: Intercultural relationships are a tapestry woven with threads of different colors and textures. Embrace the richness and complexity that comes with navigating different languages and cultures. Don't try to force your partner to conform to your way of seeing the world. Instead, learn from each other, grow together, and create a unique language of love that's all your own.

Seek Professional Guidance: Sometimes, despite our best efforts, we can get stuck in communication patterns that are difficult to break. A therapist specializing in intercultural relationships can provide valuable tools and strategies for navigating these challenges.

Love knows no bounds, no language barriers, no cultural divides. It's a universal language spoken by the heart, understood by the soul. And while language barriers can present challenges, they can also be opportunities for deeper connection, greater understanding, and a love that transcends the limitations of words. It's in those moments of vulnerability, when we struggle to express ourselves and yet are still understood, that the true magic of love shines through.

Navigating Worlds Within Worlds: A Human Journey of Cultural Adjustment

Imagine stepping onto a stage where the lights are different, the music plays a unfamiliar tune, and the very air hums with a different rhythm. That's what cultural adjustment feels like – a journey into a new world, a fascinating, sometimes bewildering, dance between your familiar self and the unknown. It's not just about swapping recipes or learning a few phrases; it's about encountering different ways of seeing the world, different ways of living, different ways of being.

This journey isn't a straight line; it's more like a winding path with unexpected turns, breathtaking vistas, and maybe a few potholes along the way. Think of it in acts, like a play unfolding:

Act I: The Honeymoon Glow: Everything sparkles! The new sights, sounds, and smells are intoxicating. You're an explorer in a vibrant, exciting land, collecting stories and experiences like precious souvenirs. Optimism is your compass, and adventure your guide.

Act II: The Fog Rolls In: The honeymoon fades, and reality bites. Suddenly, the language sounds like static, familiar routines feel alien, and even ordering a cup of coffee can feel like a Herculean task. Frustration simmers, confusion clouds your mind, and a longing for the familiar whispers in your ear. This is where the "culture shock" storm brews.

Act III: Finding Your Footing: Slowly, tentatively, you start to navigate. You learn the local lingo, discover hidden gems in the city, and maybe even make a friend or two. You're building bridges between your old world and the new, learning to appreciate the differences and finding your place within the landscape.

Act IV: A New Normal: You've found your rhythm. You may not have become a local, but you've learned to dance to the new tune. You appreciate the beauty of the differences, the richness they bring to your life. You've woven the new experiences into the fabric of your being.

Act V (and it's a big one): The Homecoming: But wait, the play isn't over! Returning home can bring its own surprises. The familiar streets might feel a little... different. You've changed, and maybe your old world has too. It's another adjustment, a reverse culture shock, as you reintegrate your experiences and find your footing once more.

What makes this journey smoother?

Think of it like packing for a trip. A well-packed bag can make all the difference:

Cultural Distance: The bigger the leap between cultures, the more preparation you need. It's like hiking a mountain versus strolling through a park.

Personality: Are you a flexible traveler or do you prefer rigid itineraries? Openness and adaptability are your best allies.

Language: Knowing the language is like having a map and compass. Even a few phrases can go a long way.

Support System: Friends, family, or even online communities can be your lifeline. They're the fellow travelers who understand the journey.

Preparation: Pre-departure training is like packing a first-aid kit. It prepares you for the unexpected bumps in the road.

Past Experiences: If you've traveled before, you've already learned a few tricks for navigating new territories.

Acculturation: Choosing your Path:

Imagine a buffet of cultural experiences. You get to choose what you take:

Integration: You savor the new flavors while still enjoying your favorites from home.
Assimilation: You embrace the new cuisine entirely, setting aside your old recipes.
Separation: You stick to the familiar dishes, preferring the tastes of home.
Marginalization: You're not sure what you want, and end up feeling lost and hungry.

Intercultural Relationships: A Duet of Cultures:

Love knows no borders, but blending cultures in a relationship is like composing a duet. It requires:

Open Communication: Talking, really listening, is the melody that keeps the song flowing.
Cultural Sensitivity: Respecting each other's cultural instruments is key to harmony.
Compromise: Sometimes, you have to adjust the tempo or key to create beautiful music together.
Mutual Support: Being each other's biggest fans makes the performance even more magical.

The World in 2025 and Beyond:

Our world is shrinking, thanks to technology. We're all becoming global citizens, connecting across cultures in ways never imagined. This means:

Virtual Connections: We can explore new cultures from our living rooms, but we need to be mindful of online nuances.

Growing Diversity: Our communities are becoming vibrant tapestries of cultures, demanding greater understanding and inclusion.

Mental Wellbeing: We're recognizing the emotional rollercoaster of cultural adjustment and seeking support when needed.

Intercultural Training: Learning how to navigate cultural differences is becoming an essential life skill.

Cultural adjustment is a deeply personal, transformative journey. It's a chance to expand your horizons, challenge your perspectives, and discover new facets of yourself. It's not always easy, but the rewards – greater empathy, deeper understanding, and a richer, more colorful life – are immeasurable.

Bridging the Divide: Weaving Understanding Through Cultural Conflict

We live in a vibrant tapestry of cultures, a global village where our lives intertwine more closely each day. This interconnectedness, while enriching, inevitably brings us face-to-face with cultural conflict. It's not about good or bad, right or wrong; it's about the beautiful, sometimes bumpy, dance of human difference. Think of it like a symphony – different instruments, playing unique melodies, coming together to create something powerful. But sometimes, a note jars, a rhythm clashes. That's where understanding cultural conflict and knowing how to navigate it becomes essential.

Why the Clash? Unraveling the Cultural Knot

Cultural conflict isn't born out of malice; it often arises from simple misinterpretations. Imagine someone offering you a gift with their left hand in some cultures, a gesture of deep disrespect. Without knowing this cultural nuance, you might feel offended, while the giver meant no harm. It's like two people speaking different languages, trying to have a conversation – frustration is inevitable without a translator.

These misunderstandings often stem from:

Lost in Translation: Body language, customs, even the tone of our voice, can carry vastly different meanings across cultures. A nod that signifies agreement in one culture might mean the opposite in another. It's a minefield of potential misinterpretations!

Communication Crossroads: Some cultures thrive on directness, laying everything on the table. Others prefer a more subtle, nuanced approach. Imagine a direct communicator trying to negotiate with someone from a culture that values indirectness – it's like two trains on a collision course.

Value Voyages: Our values, deeply ingrained from childhood, shape our worldview. Some cultures prioritize the individual, while others emphasize the collective. These differing values can lead to friction when people interact.

The Bias Blind Spot: We all carry unconscious biases, shaped by our upbringing and experiences. Ethnocentrism, the belief that our culture is superior, and stereotyping, painting entire groups with the same brush, can cloud our judgment and fuel conflict.

Building Bridges: Strategies for Harmony

So, how do we navigate these cultural currents? It's not about erasing our differences, but about understanding and respecting them. Here are some tools to build bridges:

CQ: Your Cultural Compass: Cultural intelligence isn't just about knowing facts; it's about developing the sensitivity and skills to navigate different cultural landscapes. It's like having a compass that guides you through unfamiliar territory. This involves learning about different cultures, reflecting on your own biases, and being open to new experiences.

Listen with Your Heart: Truly listening, not just waiting for your turn to speak, is crucial. Try to understand the other person's perspective, even if you don't agree with it. Empathy is the key – putting yourself in their shoes and trying to see the world through their eyes.

Open the Dialogue: Honest, respectful communication is the cornerstone of conflict resolution. Create a safe space where everyone feels heard. Focus on understanding, not winning an argument.

Respect the Dance: Acknowledge that there's no one "right" way. Different cultures have different norms, values, and ways of doing things. Embrace the diversity!

Find Common Ground: Even amidst differences, there are often shared values or goals. Focusing on these commonalities can help build bridges and create a sense of shared purpose.

Seek a Guide: Sometimes, a neutral third party, like a mediator, can help facilitate communication and find solutions. They can act as a cultural translator, helping both sides understand each other.

The Art of Flexibility: Be willing to adapt and compromise. Conflict resolution often requires give and take. It's not about winning or losing, but about finding a solution that works for everyone.

Coaching for Connection: A conflict coach can help you develop the skills to navigate cultural conflict more effectively. They can provide personalized guidance and support.

When You Need More: For deeply entrenched conflicts, seeking professional help from a therapist or counselor specializing in cross-cultural issues can be beneficial.

Stories of Harmony: Real-World Examples

Workplace Symphony: A team with members from different cultural backgrounds struggles with communication. Through cultural sensitivity training, they learn to appreciate each other's styles and create a more harmonious work environment.

Family Fusion: An intercultural couple clashes over parenting styles. By researching different approaches and having open conversations, they find a middle ground that works for their family.

Global Deal: A business negotiation between companies from different cultures stalls due to misunderstandings. By learning about each other's cultural norms, they build trust and reach a successful agreement.

A Future of Understanding:

As our world becomes increasingly interconnected, the ability to navigate cultural conflict is more important than ever. By fostering cultural intelligence, promoting empathy, and embracing open communication, we can build a future where differences are celebrated, not feared, and where conflict is an opportunity for growth and understanding. It's a future where we can all dance together in the beautiful symphony of humanity.

Weaving a Tapestry of Two Worlds: Love, Culture, and the Art of "Us"

Intercultural relationships are like vibrant tapestries, woven with threads of different colors, textures, and traditions. They tell a story of love that transcends borders, a story of two individuals embarking on a journey to create something entirely new – a shared life that honors their unique heritages while forging a unique "couple culture." It's not just about merging two identities; it's about alchemy, transforming two into a harmonious blend that resonates with both hearts. This exploration delves into the beautiful complexities of building a bicultural identity, a shared future built on mutual respect, understanding, and the courage to embrace the unknown.

More Than Just "Mix and Match": The Dynamic Dance of Bicultural Identity

Bicultural identity development isn't a static state; it's a vibrant dance, a continuous interplay of negotiation, adaptation, and creation. Imagine it as a conversation, a dialogue between two cultures unfolding within the relationship. It's about more than just understanding each other's backgrounds intellectually; it's about feeling those cultures, experiencing them, and weaving them into the fabric of your shared life. Think of it as learning a new language of love, where the vocabulary comes from both your worlds.

The "integrative" approach to bicultural identity, like a skilled conductor leading an orchestra, emphasizes the beauty of maintaining individual cultural identities while simultaneously creating a harmonious blend. It acknowledges that true richness comes from embracing the "both/and," not the "either/or." This stands in contrast to the pressure of assimilation, where one partner might feel compelled to shed their cultural skin, or separation, where cultures remain parallel lines that never truly intersect.

The Essential Ingredients: Building Blocks of a Bicultural "Us"

Several key elements contribute to the creation of a strong bicultural identity:

Respect: The Cornerstone of Connection: Respect isn't just polite acknowledgment; it's a deep, genuine curiosity about your partner's world. It's about actively listening, asking questions, and striving to see the world through their eyes. It's about recognizing that differences aren't deficits, but rather opportunities for growth and understanding.

Negotiation: The Art of Give and Take: Clashes are inevitable when two worlds collide. Negotiation isn't about winning or losing; it's about finding creative solutions that honor both perspectives. Imagine deciding where to spend the holidays. Perhaps one celebrates Christmas with a boisterous family gathering, while the other cherishes the quiet intimacy of Hanukkah. The magic lies in finding a way to honor both, perhaps by alternating celebrations or creating new, blended traditions.

Our Story: Weaving a Shared Narrative: Every couple has a story, a collection of shared jokes, inside references, and pivotal moments that define their relationship. For bicultural couples, this narrative becomes a powerful symbol of their unique journey. It's the inside joke that transcends language barriers, the blended holiday traditions, the unique way you communicate – a testament to the "us" you've created.

Language: A Bridge Between Worlds: Language is more than just words; it's a carrier of culture. Whether you choose to speak one language, both, or a beautiful hybrid, incorporating elements of each other's languages is a powerful way to stay connected to your roots. Imagine sprinkling your conversations with phrases of endearment in your partner's native tongue – a small gesture that speaks volumes.

Family: Expanding the Circle of Belonging: Integrating into each other's families can be both a joy and a challenge. Family dynamics can be complex, and cultural expectations can add another layer of nuance. Building strong relationships with in-laws and extended family is crucial, not only for your relationship but also for creating a wider circle of love and acceptance.

Society: Navigating the Outside World: Intercultural couples may face unique challenges from society, from curious questions to outright prejudice. Developing strategies for navigating these situations, whether through education, advocacy, or simply by surrounding yourselves with supportive individuals, is vital.

Challenges and Opportunities: Growing Together Through Differences

Differences in values, communication styles, and family traditions are inevitable. One partner might value collectivism, while the other prizes individualism. One might be direct in communication, while the other prefers a more subtle approach. These differences, while challenging, are also fertile ground for growth. By navigating these complexities, couples develop stronger communication skills, deeper empathy, and a richer understanding of the world.

Stories of Love: Real-Life Examples

Akiko and Michael: Akiko, from Japan, and Michael, from the US, built a life that beautifully blended their cultures. They celebrated Japanese holidays, cooked traditional meals, and spoke Japanese at home, ensuring their children grew up bilingual and bicultural, comfortable in both worlds.

Oluchi and David: Oluchi, from Nigeria, and David, from the UK, faced challenges navigating differing family expectations. Through open communication and a willingness to learn, they created a unique blend of Nigerian and British traditions in their wedding and home life, a beautiful symbol of their love story.

Building Your "Us": Practical Tips

Talk, Talk, Talk: Open, honest communication is paramount. Share your feelings, needs, and cultural perspectives with vulnerability and empathy.

Become Cultural Explorers: Immerse yourselves in each other's cultures. Read books, watch films, attend cultural events, and perhaps even travel to each other's home countries.

Embrace Flexibility: Be prepared to adapt and compromise. Rigidity has no place in an intercultural relationship.

Create Your Own Traditions: Develop unique rituals that blend elements from both cultures. This could be anything from hybrid holiday celebrations to special nicknames that transcend language barriers.

Find Your Tribe: Connect with other intercultural couples. Sharing experiences and finding support within a community can be incredibly valuable.

Embrace the Journey: Building a bicultural identity is a marathon, not a sprint. There will be highs and lows, but the journey itself is a beautiful testament to the power of love to bridge cultural divides.

Looking Ahead: A Future Woven with Diversity

In our increasingly interconnected world, intercultural relationships are becoming the norm, not the exception. As we move forward, understanding and celebrating cultural diversity will be more important than ever. Research continues to highlight the positive aspects of biculturalism, emphasizing the resilience and strength of intercultural families. We can anticipate increased support systems and resources for intercultural couples, along with a growing societal acceptance that celebrates the richness and beauty of blended cultures. The journey of building a bicultural identity is a powerful reminder that love has the power to transcend boundaries, creating something truly extraordinary – a tapestry woven with the threads of two worlds, bound by the enduring power of "us."

Part 3: Sustaining and Evolving the Bond

The Individual Within: Self-Care and Personal Growth

Weaving Two Lives, Not Merging into One: Keeping "You" in "Us"

Love. It's a beautiful dance, a shared journey, a comforting "us." But within that "us," there's always a "you" and a "me." Losing sight of those individualities can subtly erode the very foundation of a strong relationship. It's like blending two vibrant colors until they become a muddy brown – still a color, but lacking the brilliance of its original components. This isn't about creating distance; it's about ensuring your relationship enhances, not diminishes, the unique magic that makes you, you.

Think of your sense of self as the vibrant core of your being. It's the collection of your passions, quirks, dreams, and experiences – everything that makes you tick. A healthy sense of self is your personal compass, guiding you through life with confidence and purpose. When you enter a relationship, you're not signing a contract to dissolve that core; you're inviting someone to share in its radiance. Merging lives shouldn't mean merging identities. It's about two distinct individuals choosing to intertwine their journeys, each bringing their unique flavor to the mix.

So, how do you keep that flame of individuality burning bright within the context of a loving relationship? Imagine it as nurturing a garden:

Cultivate Your Own Plot: Just like a garden needs diverse plants to thrive, you need personal interests and hobbies that bring you joy outside of your relationship. Whether it's losing yourself in a novel, conquering a climbing wall, or belting out tunes in your shower, these activities are your personal sanctuaries. They're where you recharge, express yourself, and reconnect with your passions.

Tend to Your Friendships: Your friends are your chosen family, offering support, laughter, and perspectives that enrich your life beyond your romantic partnership. Nurture these connections; they're vital threads in the tapestry of your life.

Keep Dreaming: Don't let your personal goals and aspirations fade into the background. Whether it's climbing the corporate ladder, writing a novel, or learning to play the ukulele, these pursuits give you a sense of purpose and contribute to your overall self-worth. Your dreams are your own personal stars to reach for.

Speak Your Truth: Your voice matters. Don't be afraid to express your opinions, even if they differ from your partner's. Healthy relationships thrive on open communication and mutual respect, even when there's disagreement. It's about honoring your own perspective while respecting theirs.

Embrace Self-Care: You can't pour from an empty cup. Prioritize self-care activities that replenish your energy and nourish your soul. Whether it's a quiet evening with a book, a yoga class, or a walk in nature, these moments of solitude are essential for maintaining your equilibrium.

Think of self-esteem as the fertile soil in which your individuality flourishes. When you value yourself, you're more likely to attract and maintain healthy relationships. You set boundaries, communicate your needs effectively, and don't rely on your partner to validate your worth. Conversely, low self-esteem can lead to insecurity, jealousy, and a tendency to seek constant reassurance.

Let's look at a couple of real-life scenarios:

The Balancing Act: Imagine a musician deeply passionate about their art and a partner who thrives on social connections. They might find a rhythm where the musician dedicates specific evenings to their music, while the partner enjoys nights out with friends. They respect each other's needs and celebrate their differences, understanding that these individual pursuits enrich their relationship as a whole.

The Danger of Fusion: Picture a couple who become so intertwined that they lose sight of their individual identities. They neglect their friendships, abandon their hobbies, and become overly reliant on each other for validation. Over time, this fusion can lead to resentment and a sense of emptiness. The key is to rediscover those individual passions, rebuild friendships, and create space for personal growth.

Looking ahead, we can anticipate a growing emphasis on digital wellbeing. As our lives become increasingly intertwined with technology, setting boundaries around social media and prioritizing real-life connections will be crucial for maintaining individuality. We'll likely see more research focusing on the impact of online interactions on self-esteem and relationship satisfaction.

Ultimately, maintaining individuality isn't selfish; it's an act of self-love that benefits both you and your relationship. When you nurture your own unique qualities, you bring your best self to the partnership, creating a dynamic and fulfilling connection that allows both individuals to thrive. It's about weaving two lives together, not merging into one. It's about celebrating the beautiful tapestry of "us," woven with the vibrant threads of "you" and "me."

The Warm Embrace of Imperfection: Why Self-Compassion Isn't Self-Indulgent, It's Essential

Let's be honest, we're all a bit of a mess sometimes. We stumble, we fall, we say the wrong thing, we burn the dinner (again). We're human, gloriously and frustratingly so. And yet, how often do we treat ourselves with the same gentle understanding we'd offer a friend in a similar situation? Probably not often enough. That's where the magic of self-compassion comes in. It's not some fluffy, feel-good concept; it's a powerful tool for navigating the messy, beautiful, sometimes heartbreaking reality of being alive.

Imagine a close friend confessing a deep insecurity, a fear, or a recent blunder. Would you launch into a scathing critique, listing all their shortcomings? Of course not! You'd offer a comforting shoulder, a kind word, a reminder of their strengths. Self-compassion simply asks us to extend that same generosity to ourselves. It's about recognizing that imperfection is woven into the fabric of the human experience, not a personal failing. It's not about wallowing in self-pity or shirking responsibility; it's about meeting our struggles with kindness instead of judgment.

Think of it like this: you're learning to ride a bike. You're going to wobble, maybe even take a tumble. Self-compassion is the supportive voice that says, "It's okay, everyone falls! Get back on, you've got this!" Self-criticism, on the other hand, is the harsh inner voice that screams, "You're such a klutz! You'll never learn!" Which voice do you think will help you actually master the skill?

Dr. Kristin Neff, a pioneer in self-compassion research, breaks it down into three key components:

Kindness, not criticism: Imagine you've just bombed a presentation at work. Instead of replaying the disaster reel in your head, berating yourself for every perceived misstep, try this: Place a hand on your heart and whisper something like, 'This is tough, I'm feeling really disappointed. It's okay to feel this way." Acknowledge the pain without getting lost in it. Then, gently remind yourself of your strengths, your past successes, your resilience. This isn't about excusing your mistakes; it's about creating a space for learning and growth, free from the crippling weight of self-judgment.

We're all in this together: Ever feel like you're the only one struggling? Like everyone else has it figured out while you're constantly fumbling? That's the insidious power of isolation. Self-compassion reminds us that we're part of a vast, interconnected web of humanity. Everyone experiences pain, everyone makes mistakes. It's part of the deal. Recognizing this shared vulnerability can be incredibly liberating. It allows us to soften the edges of our suffering and realize we're not alone in our struggles.

Mindfulness: Being present with the mess: Mindfulness isn't about achieving some zen-like state of bliss. It's about simply being present, without judgment, with whatever arises – the good, the bad, and the ugly. It's about acknowledging your feelings without getting swept away by them. Imagine a wave crashing on the shore. Mindfulness allows you to observe the wave – its size, its power, its form – without being pulled under. It allows you to say, "I'm feeling anxious right now," without adding a layer of self-criticism on top of it. "I'm feeling anxious, and that's okay."

Now, let's talk about resilience. Life throws curveballs. It's inevitable. Self-compassion acts as a buffer against those blows. When we're self-compassionate, we're less likely to get stuck in a cycle of negative self-talk and rumination. We're more likely to pick ourselves up, dust ourselves off, and keep moving forward. It's not about pretending the pain isn't there; it's about acknowledging it, learning from it, and moving on with greater wisdom and strength.

Self-compassion also plays a crucial role in stress management. When we're stressed, that inner critic tends to get louder, amplifying our feelings of anxiety and overwhelm. Self-compassion offers a different approach. It allows us to meet our stress with kindness and understanding, reducing its intensity and helping us regain a sense of calm.

And here's the kicker: self-compassion isn't just good for you; it's good for your relationships too. When we're kinder to ourselves, we're naturally more empathetic and understanding towards others. We're less likely to project our own insecurities onto our loved ones, creating space for deeper connection and trust. It allows us to accept our own imperfections, which makes us more accepting of the imperfections of others.

So, how do you cultivate this magical quality? It's a practice, a journey, not a destination. Start small. Engage in mindful moments throughout the day. When you notice that inner critic rearing its ugly head, gently challenge it. Ask yourself, "Would I say this to a friend?" Practice self-kindness by doing things that bring you joy. Write yourself a compassionate letter. Explore guided meditations on self-compassion. If needed, seek professional support.

Self-compassion isn't selfish; it's essential. It's the foundation for a happier, healthier, more fulfilling life, both for ourselves and for those we love. It's about embracing our humanity, with all its flaws and imperfections, and recognizing that we are worthy of love and kindness, especially from ourselves.

Growing Together: A Love Story in Two Parts

Life's a winding road, isn't it? We're all on this journey of becoming, constantly evolving, learning, and reaching for our best selves. When you share that road with someone, a partner, it becomes a beautiful, sometimes bumpy, adventure in growth. It's about more than just existing side-by-side; it's about truly growing together, even as you bloom individually.

Imagine a garden. Two plants, different varieties, sharing the same soil. A healthy garden isn't about one plant overshadowing the other; it's about both thriving, supported by the shared resources and the nurturing environment. That's what a relationship focused on personal growth feels like. It's a space where each person is encouraged to reach for the sun, to stretch their roots, knowing they have a partner cheering them on.

But how do you create that kind of garden? It's not magic, though it can feel pretty magical. It starts with really seeing each other. Not just the person you fell in love with, but the person they are becoming. It means truly listening – not just hearing the words, but understanding the dreams, the fears, the whispers of their heart. It's about creating a safe space where vulnerability isn't weakness, but a bridge connecting two souls.

Think about it: have you ever felt truly heard? Like someone really got you? That feeling is powerful. It fuels us, gives us courage. And when you give that to your partner, you're giving them a gift beyond measure. You're saying, "I believe in you. I see your potential. I'm here for you, every step of the way."

Now, let's be real, life throws curveballs. Careers change, dreams shift, unexpected challenges arise. These transitions can be tough, but they can also be incredible opportunities for growth – both individually and as a couple. The key is to face them together, as a team. Imagine navigating a storm at sea. You need to communicate, adjust the sails, hold on tight. But if you do it together, you'll not only weather the storm, you'll emerge stronger, more resilient.

And sometimes, the biggest act of love is giving each other space. Think of those plants again. Sometimes, they need room to breathe, to spread their branches. It's important to nurture your own individuality, to have your own passions and friendships. This isn't about drifting apart; it's about coming back together, enriched by your experiences, bringing new perspectives and energy to the relationship.

We're living in a world that's constantly changing, and relationships are no exception. Recent research talks about "relational mindfulness" – being present in the moment, paying attention to the dynamic between you and your partner. It's about recognizing your own emotions and needs, and being attuned to theirs. It's also about finding shared meaning, those things that connect you on a deeper level – shared values, dreams for the future, or simply enjoying a quiet evening together.

Think of Sarah and Mark. Sarah always dreamed of starting her own business, a daunting leap of faith. Mark didn't just say "good luck"; he became her rock. He listened to her fears, helped her with the business plan, and even picked up extra shifts at work to support them financially. His belief in her dream became her superpower. And when her business took off, their relationship soared to new heights.

Or consider David and Lisa. David's decision to change careers initially worried Lisa. But instead of shutting down the conversation, they talked openly about their concerns. They created a budget, explored different scenarios, and ultimately, Lisa supported David's decision. His newfound fulfillment not only made him happier, it strengthened their bond.

These stories, and countless others, remind us that love isn't static. It's a living, breathing thing that requires nurturing and attention. It's about choosing to grow together, hand in hand, through all the seasons of life. It's about building a garden where both plants can flourish, creating a beautiful, vibrant tapestry of love and growth.

Finding Your "Yes": A Guide to Setting Boundaries with Grace and Grit

Ever feel like you're running on empty, constantly giving pieces of yourself away? Like your "yes" has become an automatic reflex, even when your inner voice is screaming "no"? You're not alone. We live in a world that often glorifies busyness and self-sacrifice, making boundary setting feel like a radical act. But here's the truth: boundaries aren't walls we build to keep others out; they're bridges we build to connect with our truest selves. They're about honoring our needs, protecting our energy, and ultimately, creating space for deeper, more meaningful connections.

Think of your energy like a precious garden. You wouldn't let just anyone wander in and trample your flowers, would you? Boundaries are the gentle fences that protect what's valuable, allowing your garden (your well-being) to flourish. They're not about being selfish; they're about being self-aware.

Why Boundaries Matter (More Than You Think)

We often hear that boundaries are important, but let's dive deeper into why they're so crucial:

Reclaiming Your Time: Imagine your day as a jar. Without boundaries, other people's requests, obligations, and distractions fill it up, leaving little room for what truly matters to you. Boundaries help you curate your time, ensuring there's space for your passions, your rest, and your joy.

Protecting Your Emotional Sanctuary: We've all experienced the draining feeling of being around someone who constantly complains or offloads their negativity. Emotional boundaries are like a shield, deflecting toxic energy and protecting your inner peace. They allow you to empathize without absorbing other people's emotional baggage.

Fueling Healthy Relationships: Ironically, boundaries actually strengthen relationships. When we're clear about our limits, we create a foundation of respect and understanding. It minimizes resentment and allows for more authentic, honest connections.

Boosting Self-Respect: Every time you honor a boundary, you send a powerful message to yourself: "My needs matter." It's an act of self-love that reinforces your worth and empowers you to make choices that align with your values.

Preventing the Burnout Monster: Burnout isn't just about being tired; it's about feeling depleted, disconnected, and cynical. Boundaries are your best defense. They help you manage your workload, prioritize your well-being, and maintain a sustainable pace in life's marathon.

Boundary Breakdown: It's Not One-Size-Fits-All

Boundaries aren't just about saying "no." They're about understanding your needs in different areas of your life:

Physical Space: This is about your personal bubble. Are you comfortable with hugs from acquaintances? Do you need quiet time to recharge? It's about defining your comfort zone and communicating it respectfully.

Emotional Territory: This is about protecting your feelings. Are you constantly trying to fix other people's problems? Do you absorb their negativity? It's about recognizing that you're responsible for your own emotions, not others'.

Time Management: This is about how you spend your most precious resource. Are you constantly overscheduled? Do you have time for the things that bring you joy? It's about prioritizing your commitments and saying "no" to things that drain your energy.

Possessions & Finances: This is about your stuff. Are you constantly lending things out and never getting them back? Are you comfortable discussing your finances with everyone? It's about setting clear expectations about sharing and borrowing.

Intellectual Space: This is about your thoughts and beliefs. Do you feel pressured to agree with everyone? Are you comfortable expressing dissenting opinions? It's about respecting differing viewpoints without feeling obligated to change your own.

Crafting Your Boundaries: A Step-by-Step Guide

Setting boundaries can feel daunting, but it's a skill you can develop over time:

Tune In to Yourself: Become a detective of your own feelings. When do you feel resentful, overwhelmed, or drained? These are clues that your boundaries might need adjusting.

Communicate Clearly and Kindly: Use "I" statements to express your needs without blaming others. For example, instead of saying "You're always interrupting me," try "I need some uninterrupted time to focus on this task."

Be Consistent and Firm (But Flexible): Once you've set a boundary, stick to it as much as possible. However, also be open to adjusting your boundaries as needed. Life throws curveballs, and sometimes we need to be flexible.

Prepare for Pushback: Not everyone will be thrilled about your newfound boundaries. Some people might resist or try to guilt-trip you. Remember, you have the right to protect your well-being.

Practice Self-Compassion: Setting boundaries can be emotionally challenging, especially at first. Be patient with yourself and celebrate your progress.

Boundaries in Action: Real-Life Examples

Work: "I'm happy to help with this, but I'm available after lunch."

Family: "I love you, but I need some quiet time to myself."

Friendships: "I appreciate your support, but I need to process this on my own."

Relationships: "I need some space to recharge after a long day."

The Takeaway: Your "Yes" Matters

Setting boundaries is an act of self-respect, a way of honoring your needs and creating space for what truly matters. It's about finding your "yes" – the things you wholeheartedly want to invest your time and energy in – and protecting it fiercely. It's about building those bridges to your truest self, allowing you to connect with others in a more authentic and meaningful way. And remember, you're worth it.

Rethinking Monogamy: Exploring Relationship Diversity

Let's talk about love, relationships, and all the beautiful, messy ways we connect with each other. It's not just "boy meets girl, gets married" anymore (though that's still a perfectly valid and wonderful option!). Human relationships are a vibrant tapestry, constantly evolving, and it's time we celebrate that diversity. Forget the cookie-cutter approach – love doesn't fit in a pre-made mold.

We've been told for so long that monogamy is the way, the only "normal" path. And for many, it is! There's comfort and security in that deep, exclusive bond. Think of it like your favorite cozy sweater – familiar, warm, and just right. But even within monogamy, there's room to play! Some couples are strictly committed, like two trees growing intertwined, their lives inseparable. Others practice "serial monogamy," like flipping through a series of captivating novels, each relationship a chapter in their life story. And then there's the tricky territory of emotional or social monogamy, where the lines blur and the heart's compass can sometimes point in unexpected directions. It's all about what works for you as a couple.

But what if one sweater isn't enough? What if you're drawn to the textures and colors of multiple connections? That's where things get interesting.

Open relationships are like exploring a city with a trusted companion. You have your main base, your home, but you're also free to wander, to discover new streets and hidden gems. It's about setting boundaries, communicating openly (and honestly!), and trusting that your home base will still be there when you return. It's not always easy, but for some, the freedom and exploration are worth the effort.

Then there's polyamory, which, in its simplest form, means "many loves." Imagine a garden bursting with different flowers, each beautiful in its own right. Polyamory is about having multiple loving, intimate relationships, all with the knowledge and consent of everyone involved. It's about ethical non-monogamy, where honesty and respect are the cornerstones. It can be hierarchical, like a family tree with different branches, or non-hierarchical, where all relationships are considered equal. It's complex, for sure, but for some, it's the most authentic way to love.

And let's not forget the other variations! Swinging, relationship anarchy, hybrid relationships... it's a whole alphabet soup of connection! Each one is unique, a testament to the fact that there's no one-size-fits-all when it comes to love.

We need to talk more about all of this! We need research to understand the prevalence of these different structures and how they impact our lives. We need to explore the challenges and the joys, the ups and downs, the unique dynamics of each. And most importantly, we need to ditch the judgment and embrace the diversity.

Think of real-life stories – a couple navigating the complexities of emotional connection outside their marriage, a polyamorous individual balancing multiple loving relationships, a couple deciding to open their relationship after years of monogamy. These aren't just theoretical concepts; they're real people, with real feelings, trying to figure out love in their own way.

The bottom line? Love is love. Connection is connection. And the way we choose to build our relationships is a deeply personal journey. Let's celebrate the spectrum, embrace the messy beauty of human connection, and create a world where all forms of love are valid and respected. Because at the end of the day, it's not about the label; it's about the heart.

Navigating the Heart's Expansive Landscape: Ethical Non-Monogamy in the 21st Century

Let's talk about love, relationships, and the ever-evolving ways we connect. We're diving into the world of Ethical Non-Monogamy (ENM), a relationship style that's less about "open season" and more about honest, intentional connection with multiple partners. Think of it as building a relationship ecosystem, rather than a single, isolated garden. It's not for everyone, but for those who choose this path, communication, transparency, and consent are the essential tools for cultivating healthy, thriving connections.

Communication: The Architect of Connection

Imagine trying to build a house without blueprints. Chaos, right? That's what ENM without robust communication looks like. It's not just talking – it's deep, vulnerable sharing. It's about creating a safe space to express desires, fears, boundaries, and everything in between.

Laying the Foundation: Before jumping into ENM, partners need some serious heart-to-heart time. What does ENM even mean to each of you? Are we talking polyamory (multiple loving relationships), open relationships (primarily sexual connections), or something else entirely? Getting on the same page definitionally is the first step.

Crafting the Blueprint: Think of rules and agreements not as rigid restrictions, but as a shared understanding of what feels safe and respectful. This could include guidelines about safer sex, disclosing new partners (and how!), time allocation, or emotional involvement. The process of creating these "blueprints" is communication in action!

Drawing the Boundaries: Boundaries are about respecting individual limits. Maybe one partner is comfortable with sexual connections but not romantic ones. Maybe another needs a heads-up before a new partner is introduced. These boundaries are non-negotiable; they're the lines that define each person's comfort zone.

Health and Honesty: Let's be real, safer sex talks aren't always comfortable, but they're essential. Open conversations about STIs, testing, and protection are crucial for everyone's well-being. Honesty is the best policy, especially when it comes to sexual health.

The Art of Disclosure: How and when do you tell your partner about new connections? This is a delicate dance. Some prefer full transparency, others a more curated approach. The key is finding what works for your relationship dynamic.

Regular Check-ins: The Maintenance Crew: Just like a house needs regular upkeep, so do ENM relationships. Regular check-ins, whether formal or casual, create space for sharing feelings, addressing concerns, and ensuring everyone feels heard and supported.

Communication in ENM is a living, breathing thing. It's not a one-and-done deal. Feelings change, needs evolve, and new experiences arise. Open, honest communication is the key to navigating these shifts together. This means actively listening (really listening!), sharing both the joys and the challenges, and learning how to navigate conflict constructively.

Transparency: The Open Windows of Trust

Transparency is about honesty and openness with all partners about other relationships. It's about creating an environment of trust and mutual respect.

Different Shades of Transparency: Transparency isn't one-size-fits-all. Some couples share every detail, while others prefer a more selective approach. The important thing is that everyone agrees on the level of transparency and what information will be shared.

The Power of Honesty: Transparency builds trust. When partners are honest and open, it creates a sense of safety and allows for deeper emotional intimacy. It minimizes secrecy and reduces the potential for misunderstandings.

Navigating the Tricky Bits: Let's be honest, transparency can be tough, especially when dealing with jealousy or insecurity. It requires vulnerability and a willingness to be honest with yourself and your partners. But the long-term benefits of transparency often outweigh the short-term discomfort.

Consent: The Foundation of Respect

Consent is the bedrock of ethical non-monogamy. It's not just about saying "yes" – it's about enthusiastic agreement, freely and willingly given.

Informed and Enthusiastic: Consent must be informed. Everyone involved needs all the information necessary to make an informed decision. And it should be enthusiastic! Think "hell yes!" not a hesitant "okay."

Ongoing and Revocable: Consent isn't a one-time thing. It can be withdrawn at any time. Just because someone consented yesterday doesn't mean they're obligated to today.

Boundaries and Respect: Respecting boundaries is paramount. Pressuring or coercing someone is never okay. Consent is about honoring individual limits.

Consent in the ENM Context: In ENM, consent extends to all partners. Everyone needs to be on board and actively participating. And each individual within the network has the right to set their own boundaries.

Real-World Rhythms: Case Studies in ENM

Let's look at a few scenarios to see these principles in action:

The Explorers: A couple, after years of monogamy, decides to explore ENM. They start with open conversations, researching ENM models, and defining what feels right for them. They establish safer sex agreements and disclosure protocols, committing to regular check-ins.

Navigating the Green-Eyed Monster: A woman in a polyamorous relationship experiences jealousy when her partner starts seeing someone new. Instead of bottling it up, she talks openly with her partner. They work together to address her insecurities, and her partner makes an effort to include her in some interactions with the new partner, building trust.

The Boundary Breach: A man in an open relationship agrees with his partner that they'll only have sexual relationships with others, not romantic ones. He develops feelings for someone he's seeing and crosses that line. This breach of trust highlights the importance of respecting boundaries.

The Ongoing Story of ENM

Communication, transparency, and consent are the cornerstones of ethical non-monogamy. It's a journey that requires honesty, vulnerability, and respect. ENM is not a one-size-fits-all model. What works for one relationship might not work for another. The key is to find what aligns with the values and needs of everyone involved and to keep communicating and adapting as your relationships evolve. As we move forward, we'll likely see even more nuanced understandings of ENM, shaped by evolving social norms, technology, and ongoing research. It's a conversation that's just beginning, and it's one worth having.

The Heart of It All: Navigating the Emotional Landscape of Open Relationships

Let's talk about the feels, shall we? Non-monogamy, in all its beautiful, diverse forms – polyamory, open relationships, relationship anarchy – opens up a world of love and connection beyond the traditional "one and only." But let's be real, it also opens up a Pandora's Box of emotions, especially jealousy and insecurity. These feelings aren't exclusive to non-monogamy, of course. They're part of the human experience. But in a context where multiple partners are involved, they can get...complicated. Think of it like this: your heart is a house with extra rooms, and sometimes, you're not sure who's got the key.

So, what's at the root of these prickly emotions? Jealousy, that tangled mess of fear, anger, and sadness, can pop up for different reasons. Maybe your partner forgot to mention a date with someone new (reactive jealousy – the "ouch, that stings" kind). Or maybe it's a more general unease about sharing your partner's affections (possessive jealousy – the "what if there's not enough love to go around?" worry). Insecurity, on the other hand, is often about self-doubt – the "am I good enough?" whisper in the back of your mind.

Here's the thing: society doesn't exactly prepare us for this. We're bombarded with messages about "the one," soulmates, and happily ever afters that usually involve just two people. This "mononormativity" can make anyone exploring non-monogamy feel like they're doing something wrong, even if it's exactly right for them. It's like trying to fit a square peg (your open heart) into a round hole (societal expectations).

Other contributing factors? The fear of scarcity – that love is a limited resource and if your partner gives some to someone else, there's less for you. The inevitable comparisons – "is she prettier? Smarter? More interesting?" (Spoiler alert: comparison is the thief of joy, especially in love). And of course, communication challenges. Talking about your feelings, especially the messy ones, is hard. If you can't be honest with your partner(s) about what's going on inside, those feelings can fester and grow. Unmet needs, past relationship baggage, and a lack of clear agreements and boundaries can also throw fuel on the fire.

Okay, so how do you navigate this emotional minefield? There's no magic bullet, but here are some tools to add to your relationship toolkit:

Know Thyself: Seriously, spend some time figuring out what triggers your jealousy and insecurity. Journaling, talking to a therapist (highly recommended!), or just having long conversations with yourself can help. The more you understand your own emotional landscape, the better equipped you'll be to navigate it.

Flip the Script: Jealousy and insecurity often involve negative thought patterns. "My partner is going to leave me," or "I'm not good enough." Learn to recognize these thoughts and challenge their validity. Are they really true? Or are they just stories you're telling yourself?

Talk it Out (Like, Really Talk): Open, honest communication is the lifeblood of any relationship, but it's especially crucial in non-monogamy. Create a safe space where you and your partner(s) can talk about your feelings without judgment. Listen actively, try to understand each other's perspectives, and be willing to be vulnerable.

Draw the Lines (Together): Clear agreements and boundaries are essential. What are your non-negotiables? What are you comfortable with? These agreements should cover everything from safer sex to communication protocols to how much you want to know about your partner's other relationships. And remember, these boundaries aren't set in stone. They can (and should) evolve as your relationship evolves.

Fill Your Own Cup: Self-care isn't selfish, it's essential. Make time for the things that bring you joy and make you feel good about yourself. A strong sense of self-worth is your best defense against insecurity.

Trust the Process (and Your Partner): Trust takes time to build, especially in non-monogamy. Be honest, be transparent, and follow through on your commitments. Consistency breeds trust, and trust breeds security.

Embrace the Joy (Compersion, Anyone?): Compersion, the feeling of joy for your partner's happiness in other relationships, is like the holy grail of polyamory. It might not come naturally, but it's something you can work towards. Try to reframe your thinking and focus on the positive aspects of your partner's experiences.

Get Some Help: If you're struggling, don't be afraid to seek professional help. A therapist specializing in relationship issues or non-monogamy can provide guidance, support, and tools for navigating these complex emotions.

Be Patient: Adjusting to non-monogamy takes time. Be kind to yourself and your partner(s). There will be bumps in the road. The important thing is to keep communicating, keep learning, and keep growing together.

The world of relationships is constantly changing, and non-monogamy is part of that evolution. By understanding the emotional landscape and developing the tools to navigate it, you can create loving, fulfilling connections that honor the beautiful complexity of the human heart.

The Heart of Connection: Love and Commitment in a World of Change

Love. It's a word that whispers promises of forever, yet feels as fleeting as a butterfly's wing. And commitment? Well, that's a word that's been through more makeovers than a pop star. We're living in a relationship revolution, folks, and it's time we talked about it.

Forget the dusty rulebook of yesteryear. Love isn't just about picket fences and shared bank accounts anymore (though, those can still be nice!). It's become deeply personal, a quest for your kind of happiness. Think of it like choosing your favorite flavor of ice cream – some crave the classic vanilla of traditional partnership, while others are all about the rocky road of unconventional connections.

We're all on this journey of self-discovery, and that includes our love lives. Self-love has become the essential ingredient, the foundation upon which we build relationships. It's like learning to swim before diving into the deep end – you need to know your own strength before you can truly connect with someone else. Sure, it can make us a little more hesitant to compromise, but isn't it better to enter a relationship whole, rather than seeking someone to complete us?

Then there's technology, the love guru and relationship wrecker all rolled into one. Dating apps have turned finding a partner into a digital treasure hunt, offering a seemingly endless supply of potential matches. But let's be real, swiping left and right can feel more like shopping than falling in love. And those perfectly curated online profiles? They often set the bar so high that reality can't help but disappoint. Plus, technology's constant buzz can blur the lines between "me time" and "we time," making true intimacy a little harder to find.

But love, in its infinite wisdom, refuses to be confined. The traditional, storybook image of romance is being rewritten. We're embracing the beautiful spectrum of LGBTQ+ relationships, recognizing that love doesn't care about gender or labels. And concepts like polyamory are nudging the boundaries of what we consider "normal," reminding us that love can take many forms.

Commitment, too, is getting a modern makeover. The white dress and diamond ring aren't the only symbols of "forever" anymore. Marriage rates are dipping, while cohabitation is on the rise. Some couples are ditching the formal ceremony altogether, choosing instead to express their commitment through shared experiences, personal vows, or simply the quiet understanding of two souls intertwined.

We're also seeing the rise of "serial monogamy," where we hop from one exclusive relationship to the next. It's like test-driving different cars before finally settling on the perfect one. But does this constant search for "the one" prevent us from truly investing in the relationship we're in?

And let's not forget the digital age's impact on commitment. While technology can keep us connected, it can also open doors to temptation. Infidelity in the digital realm can be just as hurtful as the traditional kind, and the constant availability of potential partners can make it harder to stay committed.

So, what does the future hold for love and commitment? It's all about you. Relationships will become even more personalized, reflecting our individual needs and desires. Fluidity and flexibility will be key, as we learn to navigate the ever-changing landscape of life and love. Technology will continue to shape our experiences, for better or worse. And emotional intimacy will be the gold standard, the connection we crave above all else.

Think of "conscious uncoupling" as a sign of the times. Even breakups are getting a compassionate makeover, focusing on personal growth and minimizing the emotional fallout. And social media? It's a double-edged sword. It can fuel jealousy and insecurity, but it can also be a powerful tool for connection and support. Even polyamorous relationships, with their open and honest approach to love, are becoming more visible, challenging our preconceived notions of what it means to be in love. Ultimately, the future of love and commitment is a choose-your-own-adventure story. We're the authors, rewriting the narrative of relationships one connection at a time. It's a wild ride, full of twists and turns, but one thing's for sure: the human need for connection will always be at the heart of it all.

Love, Sex, and Power: Relationships in the #MeToo Era

Beyond "No": A Heart-to-Heart on Consent

Let's talk about consent. It's a word we hear a lot, but do we really get it? Think of it less like a legal checklist and more like a conversation – a continuous, open, and honest exchange between people who respect each other. It's about more than just saying "no," it's about actively saying "yes," and feeling genuinely good about it.

Imagine you're offered a slice of cake. If you light up and say "Yes, please!" that's enthusiastic consent. If you just shrug and say "Sure, whatever," that's not exactly a resounding "yes," is it? And if you don't say anything at all, or even worse, look uncomfortable, that definitely doesn't mean you want cake. Consent in intimate moments is the same. It's not about what you don't say, it's about the genuine enthusiasm you do express.

Think of it like this: every intimate moment is a brand new conversation. Just because you enjoyed cake yesterday doesn't mean you want it today. You have the right to change your mind, every single time. Maybe you're not feeling well, maybe you're stressed, maybe you just don't feel like it – and that's perfectly okay. Your "yes" needs to be real, in the present moment, and it can be taken back at any time.

Now, let's be real, talking about this stuff can be awkward. We're often taught that sex is this unspoken, mysterious thing, but honestly, open communication is the biggest turn-on. Imagine how much better an experience would be if everyone involved felt comfortable and respected.

No guessing games, no pressure, just clear communication and genuine connection.

And here's the thing: consent isn't just about sex. It's about respecting boundaries in every aspect of life. It's about understanding that everyone has the right to say "no" to anything that makes them uncomfortable, whether it's a hug, a touch on the arm, or something more intimate.

We've come a long way in our understanding of consent, thanks in part to movements like #MeToo, which bravely brought these conversations into the light. But we still have work to do. We need to create a world where everyone understands what consent truly means, where everyone feels empowered to speak up, and where everyone respects each other's boundaries.

So, let's ditch the awkward silences and embrace open, honest communication. Let's listen to each other, respect each other, and create a culture where every "yes" is truly enthusiastic. Because at the end of the day, consent is about more than just sex – it's about respect, it's about trust, and it's about treating each other like human beings. And that's something we all deserve.

Let's talk about power. Not the kind that lets you move mountains, but the kind that simmers beneath the surface of our relationships, coloring everything from who chooses the restaurant to bigger life decisions. It's a tricky thing, this power dynamic, because it's not always a villain with a mustache twirling in the corner. Sometimes, it's a quiet hum, an unspoken understanding, a subtle lean in one direction.

Think about it: power exists in every connection we have, from the barista who remembers your complicated coffee order (and thus, holds a tiny bit of power over your caffeine fix) to the dynamics within our families, friendships, and especially, our romantic partnerships. And while power itself isn't inherently bad – sometimes, someone needs to take the lead – it's when things get unbalanced that problems start to brew. That's when a relationship, instead of being a source of joy and support, can become a breeding ground for resentment, manipulation, and even abuse.

Now, how does this power tango play out in real life? Well, it's a mix of a lot of things. We're talking about old-fashioned gender roles that still whisper in our ears, even if we try to ignore them. We're talking about who controls the purse strings, because let's face it, money talks. We're talking about emotional needs, and how sometimes, needing someone just a little too much can tip the scales. We're talking about social standing, who knows who, who has that impressive title. Even something as simple as who has the most information about a particular topic can shift the power balance. And yes, let's not forget, physical strength can unfortunately be a factor, especially in abusive situations – this is never okay, and help is always available. Even the way we communicate – are we assertive, passive, or maybe even a bit aggressive? – plays a role in this intricate dance.

So, how do you know if the power balance in your relationship is off-kilter? It's not always a neon sign flashing "Danger!" Sometimes, it's more like a nagging feeling. Maybe one person always gets to choose what you do on date night. Maybe one person's opinion always seems to carry more weight. Maybe you feel like you're constantly walking on eggshells. Maybe you're starting to feel isolated from your friends and family. Or maybe, just maybe, you're starting to doubt your own gut feelings, like you're going a little crazy. This is a huge red flag. It's called gaslighting, and it's a form of manipulation.

The good news is, power imbalances aren't set in stone. We can change them. It takes courage, honesty, and a willingness to have some tough conversations. It means talking openly about how you both feel about the power dynamic in your relationship. It means learning to truly listen to each other, even when it's uncomfortable. It means making decisions together, not just one person calling all the shots. It means being transparent about finances, even if it feels awkward. It means respecting each other's boundaries, big and small. And it means supporting each other's dreams and goals, not holding each other back.

Sometimes, even with the best intentions, couples get stuck. That's where a therapist can be a lifesaver. They can help you untangle the knots of unhealthy patterns and guide you toward a more balanced and fulfilling relationship.

Think of it this way: a healthy relationship is like a seesaw where both people are sitting at the same height, laughing together. It might wobble a bit sometimes, but it's always striving for equilibrium. It's a place where both voices are heard, both needs are valued, and both people feel empowered to be their true selves. And that, my friends, is a beautiful thing.

Navigating the Intimacy Maze: Talking About Sex, Boundaries, and Consent

Let's be real, talking about sex, boundaries, and consent can feel like navigating a minefield. It's awkward, sometimes uncomfortable, and often shrouded in a mix of societal baggage and personal anxieties. But guess what? Open and honest communication is the key to healthy, fulfilling relationships. Think of it as building a bridge to intimacy, one conversation at a time. This isn't just about avoiding awkward silences; it's about creating a space where everyone feels respected, understood, and empowered.

Why Does This Stuff Feel So Hard?

Let's break down why these conversations can be so tough:

The "Sex Talk" Hangover: Society often treats sex like a dirty secret. We're raised with a mix of misinformation, shame, and hushed tones, making open discussion feel taboo. It's like trying to dance gracefully while wearing lead boots.

Education Gaps: Many of us didn't get the sex education we deserved. We might lack the vocabulary to express our needs or the understanding of healthy sexual dynamics. It's like trying to build a house without the blueprints.

Fear of Rejection: Putting yourself out there, sharing your desires and boundaries, can feel incredibly vulnerable. Nobody wants to be judged or rejected, especially when it comes to something so personal.

Power Plays: Relationships aren't always equal. Power imbalances can make it difficult for one person to express their needs or say "no" without fear of repercussions.

Consent Confusion: Consent isn't a checkbox; it's an ongoing conversation. There are so many misconceptions floating around, from thinking silence equals "yes" to believing consent can't be withdrawn. We need to ditch these outdated ideas and embrace a more nuanced understanding.

Vulnerability Hang-Up: Talking about sex requires vulnerability, and that can be scary! It means opening yourself up and risking emotional exposure. It's like standing on a stage with a spotlight, except you're sharing your innermost self.

Building a Bridge to Open Communication:

So, how do we overcome these hurdles and start having these crucial conversations? Here's your toolkit:

Trust: The Foundation: Trust is the bedrock of any intimate relationship. It's built over time through consistent respect, honesty, and empathy. Think of it as laying the foundation for your communication bridge.

Timing is Everything: Don't try to have these conversations when you're stressed, tired, or distracted. Choose a time and place where you both feel relaxed and comfortable. Think cozy and private, not rushed and public.

Baby Steps: Start with the less intimidating stuff and gradually work your way up to more sensitive topics. It's like learning to swim – you start in the shallow end before diving into the deep.

"I" Statements are Your Friend: Express your feelings and needs using "I" statements. For example, "I feel more connected when..." or "I'd love to explore...". This avoids blame and encourages open dialogue.

Listen Up: Really listen to what your partner is saying, both verbally and nonverbally. Ask clarifying questions and show genuine empathy. It's not just about waiting for your turn to talk; it's about understanding their perspective.

Honesty is the Best Policy (Even When It's Hard): Be honest about your thoughts and feelings, even if they're uncomfortable. Authenticity breeds trust and deeper connection.

Respect the Boundaries: Always respect your partner's boundaries, even if you don't understand them. Everyone has the right to say "no," and that should always be honored.

Discomfort is Normal: These conversations can be awkward, and that's okay! Acknowledge the discomfort and embrace it as an opportunity for growth.

Knowledge is Power: Educate yourselves! Read books, explore reputable websites, or talk to a therapist specializing in sex therapy. The more you know, the more confident you'll feel.

Consider a Guide: If you're struggling to communicate effectively, consider seeking professional help. A therapist can provide a safe space to explore your concerns and develop healthy communication skills.

Talking About Sex, Boundaries, and Consent – The Nitty Gritty:

Sex: Be specific about what you enjoy. Focus on the positive ("I love it when...") rather than the negative ("I don't like..."). Explore fantasies together (if you're both comfortable) and discuss sexual health openly.

Boundaries: Communicate your boundaries clearly. Remember, boundaries can be physical, emotional, or sexual, and they can change over time. Regularly check in with each other. And remember, it's always okay to say "no."

Consent: Consent is enthusiastic, ongoing, and freely given. It's not the absence of "no," but the presence of a clear "yes." It can be withdrawn at any time. Never assume consent.

Case Studies: Real-Life Scenarios:

New Adventures: A couple wants to try something new, but one partner is hesitant. Open communication, active listening, and respecting boundaries are key. They explore the hesitation, address concerns, and find a compromise.

Changing Comfort Levels: During intimacy, one partner becomes uncomfortable. They express this, and the other partner immediately stops, checks in, and respects their right to withdraw consent.

Desire Discrepancies: A couple has different levels of desire. They talk openly about their needs and find creative ways to meet each other's needs while respecting boundaries.

The Future of Consent:

Our understanding of consent is constantly evolving. We're moving towards:

Affirmative Consent: Actively seeking and receiving explicit verbal or nonverbal "yes" at each stage.
Contextual Consent: Recognizing that consent can vary depending on the situation.
Trauma-Informed Approaches: Understanding how past trauma can impact consent.
Digital Consent: Navigating consent in the digital age (sexting, sharing images, etc.).

The Ongoing Conversation:

These conversations aren't a one-and-done thing. They need to be ongoing, evolving as your relationship grows. Regular check-ins and open communication are essential for maintaining mutual understanding and ensuring everyone feels respected and safe. It's a journey, not a destination.

Finding Your Footing Again: A Journey of Healing After Sexual Harassment and Assault

Sexual harassment and assault – these aren't just words, they're experiences that shatter lives. They leave deep wounds, invisible to the casual observer, but agonizingly real to those who carry them. This isn't about statistics (though the numbers are staggering). This is about Sarah, the college student whose laughter now catches in her throat. This is about David, the professional whose confident stride has become hesitant. This is about the countless individuals whose stories often go unheard, buried beneath layers of shame and fear.

Imagine your world suddenly tilting on its axis. That's what sexual harassment and assault can do. It robs you of your sense of safety, the very foundation upon which we build our lives. It whispers insidious lies about your worth, your body, your very being. And the psychological fallout? It can feel like a storm raging inside.

Let's talk honestly about what that storm might look like. There's no single "right" way to feel after something like this. Your experience is your own, valid and unique. But some common threads weave through these experiences. Think of them not as diagnoses, but as echoes of trauma:

   The Uninvited Guest: PTSD. Flashbacks aren't just memories; they're visceral replays, hijacking your present with the terror of the past. Sleep becomes a battlefield of nightmares, and everyday sounds can trigger a jolt of fear.

   The Constant Companion: Anxiety. A knot in your stomach that never quite unravels. The world, once a place of possibilities, now feels like a minefield of potential threats. Panic attacks can strike without warning, leaving you breathless and terrified.

   The Heavy Blanket: Depression. The joy drains from life, leaving behind a landscape of gray. Simple tasks feel monumental, and the desire to connect with others fades.

   The Whispering Liar: Shame and Guilt. This is perhaps the cruelest trick of trauma. It whispers that you are to blame, that you are somehow responsible for what happened.

But hear this, loud and clear: You are not to blame. The responsibility lies solely with the perpetrator.

The Shattered Mirror: Self-Esteem and Body Image. Your body, once a source of strength and identity, can become a battleground. Feelings of violation and disgust can make it hard to look in the mirror, let alone feel comfortable in your own skin.

The Broken Bridge: Intimacy and Relationships. Trust, once freely given, now feels like a precious, fragile thing. Intimacy can become fraught with fear, making it hard to connect with others on a meaningful level.

The False Comfort: Substance Abuse. The urge to numb the pain, to silence the screaming inside, can be overwhelming. But this is a temporary fix, a band-aid on a deep wound. True healing requires facing the pain, not escaping it.

The Detachment: Dissociation. Feeling disconnected from yourself, your body, your surroundings – this is a common response to overwhelming trauma. It's like your mind is trying to protect you by checking out.

Sarah's story isn't unique. She's a composite of so many survivors. The flashbacks, the withdrawal, the self-blame – these are all echoes of a trauma that needs to be acknowledged and addressed. But Sarah's story also offers hope. She sought help. She found a therapist who understood her experience. And slowly, painstakingly, she began to heal.

You are not alone. Help is available.

There are people who understand what you're going through, who can offer a lifeline in the darkness.

Therapy: Imagine therapy as a gentle hand guiding you through the tangled forest of your emotions. A skilled therapist can help you process the trauma, challenge negative thoughts, and develop healthy coping mechanisms.

Support Groups: There's power in shared experience. Connecting with other survivors can be incredibly validating, a reminder that you're not alone in this.

Hotlines: Need someone to talk to right now? Hotlines like RAINN offer immediate, confidential support. They're there for you 24/7.

Medical Care: Taking care of your physical health is just as important as taking care of your mental health. Seek medical attention after an assault, both for immediate needs and for long-term well-being.

Legal Assistance: Navigating the legal system can be daunting, but you don't have to do it alone. Legal aid organizations can help you understand your rights and options.

Advocacy Organizations: These organizations are champions for survivors, providing resources, support, and advocating for change.

Online Resources: The internet can be a valuable source of information and support. But be sure to choose reputable websites, like those of RAINN or the National Alliance to End Sexual Violence.

Healing is a journey, not a race. There will be good days and bad days. Be patient with yourself. Be kind to yourself. And remember, you are stronger than you think.

You are not defined by what happened to you. You are a survivor. And your journey to healing, to reclaiming your life, is a testament to your strength and resilience.

The Dance of Intimacy: Physical and Emotional Connection

The Silent Symphony: How Touch Speaks Volumes

We often think of intimacy in terms of grand gestures and whispered words, but sometimes, the most profound connections are forged in silence, through the simple language of touch. Beyond the charged energy of sexual intimacy, lies a vast and often overlooked world of non-sexual touch, a subtle yet powerful force that shapes our relationships, our well-being, and even our very understanding of ourselves. It's a language we learn from the moment we're born, a primal dialogue that speaks volumes where words fall short.

Imagine a newborn, cradled in their mother's arms. The gentle pressure, the warmth, the feeling of being held – this is the infant's first conversation, a wordless exchange of love and security. This initial experience lays the foundation for our lifelong relationship with touch, influencing how we connect with others and how we perceive the world around us. It's a biological imperative, woven into our DNA.

Our skin, the body's largest organ, isn't just a protective layer; it's a vast network of sensory receptors, each one a tiny messenger carrying information to the brain. A light caress, a firm handshake, a comforting pat on the back – each touch tells a story, triggering a cascade of hormonal responses. Oxytocin, the "love hormone," floods our system, fostering feelings of connection, trust, and belonging. Endorphins, our natural painkillers and mood elevators, soothe our anxieties and lift our spirits. Touch, in its myriad forms, is a powerful elixir, a natural remedy for the stresses of modern life.

But touch isn't just about biology; it's deeply psychological. It's the language of empathy, the unspoken reassurance that says, "I'm here for you." A hand squeezed in support during a difficult moment, a playful nudge between friends, a comforting hug after a loss – these seemingly small gestures can speak volumes, conveying emotions that words often struggle to capture. The absence of touch, on the other hand, can be deafening, signaling distance, rejection, or a lack of connection.

Think about the different ways touch manifests in our lives. A child seeking comfort from a parent, a teenager sharing a secret with a close friend, a couple cuddling on the couch after a long day – touch weaves its way through the tapestry of our relationships, strengthening the bonds that connect us. It's the silent glue that holds families together, the spark that ignites romantic passion, and the bridge that connects us to our friends and communities.

This need for touch isn't something we outgrow. It evolves as we move through different stages of life, but it never truly disappears. From the playful tickles of childhood to the comforting embraces of old age, touch remains a vital part of the human experience. In a world that often feels increasingly disconnected, the power of touch is more important than ever.

Of course, navigating the world of touch requires sensitivity and awareness. Cultural norms vary, and personal boundaries must always be respected. What feels comforting to one person might feel intrusive to another. It's crucial to pay attention to nonverbal cues, to ask for consent, and to be mindful of the context in which touch occurs.

But despite these complexities, the fundamental truth remains: touch is essential for our well-being. It nourishes our bodies, soothes our minds, and strengthens our connections with others. It's a language we all speak, a silent symphony of connection that reminds us that we are not alone. So, let's embrace the power of touch, not just in our romantic relationships, but in all aspects of our lives. Let's offer a comforting hand, a supportive hug, a playful pat on the back. Let's rediscover the simple joy of human connection, one touch at a time.

The Quiet Symphony of Connection: Weaving Emotional Intimacy

Emotional intimacy. It's not a thunderous declaration of love, but the quiet symphony played between two hearts that understand each other's rhythm. Imagine two trees, their roots intertwined beneath the soil, sharing nutrients and weathering storms together. That's the essence of emotional intimacy – a deep, nourishing connection that goes beyond the surface. It's the feeling of being seen, truly seen, by another person, flaws and all, and knowing you're loved anyway.

This isn't about reciting your life story; it's about sharing the meaning behind the story. It's about letting someone glimpse the landscape of your soul – the sun-drenched meadows of joy, the shadowy valleys of fear, and the quiet, whispering forests of your dreams. And in return, being invited into theirs.

Think of it like this: physical intimacy is the dance, but emotional intimacy is the music. You can have the steps down perfectly, but without the melody, it's just movement, not magic.

So, how do we compose this beautiful melody?

The Building Blocks of Heart-to-Heart:

Unveiling Yourself (Self-Disclosure): It's not just about spilling secrets; it's about sharing the why behind them. "I had a bad day" is information. "I had a bad day because I felt overlooked in the meeting, and it triggered old insecurities about my value" is vulnerability. It's the difference between showing someone a picture and telling them the story behind it.

Holding Space (Mutual Respect and Acceptance): Imagine a cozy armchair, a place where you can relax and be yourself, no judgment, no critiques, just acceptance. That's what you create for each other. It's about cherishing the quirks, understanding the imperfections, and offering a safe haven for their authentic self.

The Bedrock of Belief (Trust): Trust is the oxygen of emotional intimacy. It's knowing that your vulnerabilities won't be weaponized, your secrets are safe, and your heart is held with care. It's built brick by brick, through consistent actions and unwavering support.

Walking in Their Shoes (Empathy and Understanding): Empathy isn't just listening; it's feeling with the other person. It's about climbing into their emotional shoes and walking a mile in their experience, even if you don't agree with their perspective. It's saying, "I hear you, I see you, and I understand."

Daring to Be Seen (Vulnerability): This is the scariest and most rewarding part. It's about lowering your defenses, taking off the masks, and revealing your true self, even the parts you're not proud of. It's like standing naked in the sunlight – terrifying, but also liberating.

Responding with Heart (Responsiveness): It's not just about hearing; it's about responding. It's acknowledging their emotions, validating their feelings, and showing that you care. A simple "That sounds really tough, I'm here for you" can be more powerful than you know.

Shared Adventures (Shared Activities and Experiences): Life isn't just about the big moments; it's about the small ones, the shared laughter, the inside jokes, the quiet moments of connection. It's about building a shared history, a tapestry woven with shared experiences.

Nurturing the Flame:

Emotional intimacy isn't a destination; it's a journey. It requires constant tending, like a delicate flame. Communication is key – honest, open, and respectful communication. It's about learning each other's love languages, understanding their needs, and expressing your own in a way that can be heard.

The Roadblocks:

Life throws curveballs. Fear, past hurts, communication breakdowns, stress – they can all create roadblocks on the path to intimacy. Sometimes, professional guidance can help navigate these challenges and rediscover the path to connection.

A Symphony for Two:

Emotional intimacy is a gift, a treasure to be cherished and nurtured. It's the quiet symphony that plays between two souls, a melody of understanding, acceptance, and love. It's the heart of connection, the foundation of a strong and lasting relationship. And it's a song worth singing together.

Let's talk about intimacy. Not just the boom-chicka-boom kind, though that's definitely part of the conversation. I'm talking about the real, deep-down, heart-to-heart connection that makes a relationship truly sing. Think of it like a garden: you can't just toss some seeds in the dirt and expect roses. You've got to nurture it, tend to it, and give it the right conditions to flourish. Intimacy is the same way – it needs both physical and emotional nourishment to really thrive.

These two aren't separate entities, either. They're more like dance partners, each influencing the other. Imagine trying to waltz with someone who's miles away emotionally – awkward, right? Similarly, a purely physical connection without emotional depth can feel...empty. It's like eating a beautifully decorated cake that tastes like cardboard. Looks good, but leaves you unsatisfied.

Physical intimacy is more than just sex. It's the little things: holding hands while watching a movie, a quick kiss on the cheek, cuddling on the couch. These small gestures release oxytocin, that magical "love hormone" that makes you feel all warm and fuzzy inside. It's like a secret language of touch, communicating love and support without saying a word.

Emotional intimacy is where you share your inner world: your hopes, your fears, your goofy quirks. It's about feeling safe enough to be your true, authentic self, flaws and all, and knowing that your partner will accept you. It's built on trust, vulnerability, and really listening to each other – not just waiting for your turn to talk.

So, how do you cultivate this beautiful garden of intimacy?

For the Emotional Blooms:

Date Nights (and I mean real date nights): Put away the phones, turn off the TV, and focus on each other. Talk, laugh, and rediscover why you fell in love in the first place. It's like watering your plants – essential for growth.

Honest Conversations (even the tough ones): Communication is key. Be open and honest about your feelings, even when it's uncomfortable. Active listening is crucial here – really try to understand your partner's perspective. It's like pruning your rose bushes – sometimes you have to cut away the dead stuff to let new growth flourish.

Empathy (walk a mile in their shoes): Try to see things from your partner's point of view, even if you don't agree. Validate their feelings, even if you don't understand them. It's like giving your plants the right amount of sunlight – understanding their needs is crucial.

Vulnerability (it's scary, but worth it): Sharing your vulnerabilities can be scary, but it's also incredibly rewarding. It creates a deeper connection and shows your partner that you trust them. It's like planting delicate flowers – they require extra care, but their beauty is worth the effort.

Appreciation (sprinkle some love): Don't forget to tell your partner how much you appreciate them. Small gestures of appreciation can go a long way. It's like fertilizing your plants – a little boost can make a big difference.

For the Physical Blossoms:

Non-Sexual Touch (the little things that count): Hold hands, cuddle, give each other massages. These small gestures can make a big difference in creating a sense of closeness. It's like giving your plants a gentle mist – refreshing and revitalizing.

Communication (yes, even about this): Talk to your partner about your physical needs and desires. Be open and honest about what you like and what makes you feel good. It's like reading the instructions on the seed packet – knowing what your plants need is essential.

Romance (set the mood): Create a romantic atmosphere for intimacy. Light some candles, put on some music, and make it special. It's like creating the perfect environment for your plants to thrive.

Presence (be in the moment): When you're physically intimate, be present in the moment. Focus on the sensations and enjoy the experience. It's like savoring the beauty of your blooming flowers – take the time to appreciate it.

Remember, intimacy is a journey, not a destination. It takes time, effort, and a willingness to be vulnerable. But the rewards – a deep, loving, and fulfilling relationship – are definitely worth it. It's like tending to a garden – it takes work, but the beauty you create is immeasurable.

Juggling Act: Balancing Career and Relationships

Love in the Age of the Overwhelmed: Reclaiming Romance in a Hectic World

Let's be honest, life these days feels like a runaway train. We're all juggling careers, family, social obligations, and the ever-present buzz of technology. In the midst of this whirlwind, our love lives can often feel like they're getting the short end of the stick. We tell ourselves we'll "make time" for romance, but somehow, "later" never seems to arrive. The truth is, love doesn't just magically flourish; it needs tending, just like any other precious thing in our lives. So, how do we carve out space for connection amidst the chaos? It's about more than just scheduling; it's about a fundamental shift in how we approach time and prioritize what truly matters.

The Time Thief:

We're living in the "always-on" era. Our phones ping with work emails at all hours, the pressure to be constantly available is immense, and the lines between our professional and personal lives have become so blurred they're practically invisible. It's no wonder our relationships are feeling the strain. We're exhausted, stressed, and often feel like we're running on empty. How can we possibly nurture a loving relationship when we barely have time to shower, let alone connect with our partners?

The Relationship Rollercoaster:

Think of your relationship like a plant. If you neglect it, it withers. It's not rocket science. Studies confirm what our hearts already know: a lack of work-life balance is a relationship killer. When we're constantly stressed and stretched thin, our partners often bear the brunt of it. We become short-tempered, distant, and emotionally unavailable. It's a recipe for disconnection, resentment, and ultimately, heartbreak.

Reclaiming Your Time, Reclaiming Your Love:

So, what's the secret to finding time for love in a world that seems determined to steal it? It's not about finding more time (because let's face it, who has that?), it's about making the time we do have count.

Date Night, Not Just a Night Out: Instead of just "going out," schedule intentional date nights. Put it in your calendar, treat it like a crucial meeting, and for heaven's sake, put your phones away! Focus on each other. Really listen. Reconnect.

Boundary Patrol: This is crucial. Set clear boundaries between work and personal life. Turn off notifications after a certain time. Resist the urge to check emails on weekends. It's hard, but it's essential. Your sanity (and your relationship) will thank you.

The Art of Delegation: Learn to say no. You don't have to do everything. Delegate tasks at work, outsource chores if you can afford it, and don't be afraid to ask for help. Freeing up even a little time can make a world of difference.

Little Moments, Big Impact: Romance doesn't have to be grand gestures. It's often the little things that matter most. A surprise text, a shared laugh, a cuddle on the couch – these small moments of connection can add up to something truly special.

Rituals of Connection: Create rituals that bring you closer. Maybe it's making coffee together in the morning, going for a walk after dinner, or having a weekly "unplugged" evening. These shared moments create a sense of intimacy and connection.

Presence Over Productivity: When you are with your partner, be present. Put away your phone, make eye contact, and truly listen. Give them your undivided attention. It's the most valuable gift you can give.

Fun and Games: Remember when you first started dating? You probably did fun, spontaneous things together. Don't let that spark die! Keep the sense of adventure alive. Try new restaurants, explore new places, and do things that make you laugh.

The Relationship Check-Up: Just like you go to the doctor for regular check-ups, your relationship needs attention too. Talk openly and honestly about your needs and expectations. Are you both feeling loved and appreciated? Are there areas where you can improve?

Real Life, Real Love:

John and Sarah, two high-powered executives, were so busy climbing the corporate ladder that their relationship was crumbling beneath them. They were like ships passing in the night. Finally, they realized something had to change. They started scheduling "connection time" – not just dates, but dedicated time to talk, listen, and just be together. They also became more mindful of their work boundaries, refusing to let their jobs completely consume their lives. Slowly but surely, they started to reconnect. They rediscovered the joy of being together, and their love blossomed again.

The Takeaway:

Love isn't a destination; it's a journey. It requires effort, commitment, and a willingness to prioritize it, even when life gets crazy. By reclaiming our time, setting boundaries, and focusing on connection, we can create loving, fulfilling relationships that thrive, even in the age of the overwhelmed. It's not about finding the time; it's about making the time count. And that's an investment that's always worth making.

Let's face it, juggling work, life, and love in today's world feels like trying to keep a dozen plates spinning. We're all striving for that elusive "work-life balance," but often, it feels more like a "work-life scramble." Especially for couples, the struggle is real. Who does what? How do we avoid resentment building up like unwashed dishes? It's a conversation every couple needs to have, and let's be honest, it's not always an easy one.

Think about it: we're bombarded with images of perfect partnerships, where everything is split 50/50. But life isn't a perfectly symmetrical pie chart. Traditional gender roles still linger, even if we like to think we've moved past them. And let's not forget the soul-crushing reality of dual-income households, where "work" bleeds into "life" thanks to our ever-present phones. It's exhausting! So, how do we actually do this?

First, ditch the idea of "equality" and embrace "fairness." Equality sounds great on paper, but fairness acknowledges that life throws curveballs. One partner might have a killer promotion that demands extra hours, while the other is dealing with a sick parent. Fairness means recognizing these differences and adjusting the workload accordingly. It's about what's right for your relationship, not what looks good on Instagram.

Now, let's get practical. Imagine your household chores as a giant, messy to-do list. Instead of letting it overwhelm you, break it down. Who enjoys cooking? Who secretly loves organizing the garage? Playing to each other's strengths isn't just efficient, it actually makes things more enjoyable (or at least less painful). And don't forget the invisible labor – the mental load of remembering birthdays, scheduling doctor's appointments, and keeping track of school events. That needs to be acknowledged and shared too.

Communication is key. Seriously, talk about this stuff! Not when you're both stressed and snapping at each other, but during a calm moment, maybe over a glass of wine (or your beverage of choice). Be honest about your needs and limitations. Listen to your partner without getting defensive. This isn't a competition; it's a collaboration. And remember, things change. Kids grow, jobs shift, life throws us curveballs. Regular check-ins are essential to make sure the balance (or the scramble) is still working.

Technology can be both a blessing and a curse. Shared calendars can be lifesavers, chore-tracking apps can bring some much-needed order to the chaos, and online grocery shopping? Game changer! But don't let technology take over your life. Set boundaries. Designated work hours, "no phone zones," and "no phone times" are crucial. Protect your "couple time" like it's a precious jewel. Put the phones away and actually connect. Remember why you fell in love in the first place?

And finally, don't be afraid to ask for help. If your budget allows, outsourcing tasks like cleaning or gardening can free up valuable time and energy. It's not a sign of weakness; it's a smart investment in your relationship.

Real life isn't a perfectly curated Instagram feed. There will be messy moments, disagreements, and times when the plates come crashing down. But by focusing on open communication, fairness, and a willingness to adapt, you can navigate the work-life scramble together and build a partnership that's strong, supportive, and truly balanced – in a way that works for you.

Love and Politics: Navigating Relationships in a Divided World

When Left Meets Right (or Not): Love, Politics, and the Art of Peaceful Coexistence

Let's be honest, pillow talk can get interesting these days. It's not just about who did the dishes anymore. Increasingly, couples are finding themselves on opposite sides of the political spectrum, turning date night into debate night. And while a little healthy disagreement can spice things up, the current political climate has turned up the heat, leaving many wondering if love can truly conquer all, even when "all" includes deeply ingrained political ideologies.

We all know that shared values are the glue that holds relationships together. It's that feeling of "Hey, you get me!" But what happens when those core beliefs clash, especially when they manifest as opposing political views? Can you really cuddle up with someone who thinks your favorite news channel is the enemy?

The truth is, politics has become incredibly personal. It's not just about tax brackets and trade agreements anymore. It's about who we are, what we believe, and how we see the world. So, when political differences arise in a relationship, it can feel like a fundamental disconnect, a challenge to the very foundation of your connection.

Imagine this: Sarah, a passionate advocate for social justice, finds herself falling for Mark, a staunch fiscal conservative. Their first few dates are bliss, filled with laughter and shared interests. But then, the conversation turns to healthcare, and suddenly, the air thickens. Sarah's fiery passion clashes with Mark's pragmatic approach, and they find themselves locked in a heated debate. Is this a deal-breaker? Can they find a way to bridge this divide, or is their budding romance doomed to fizzle out?

The research isn't exactly encouraging. Studies show a growing trend of "political homophily" – basically, birds of a feather flocking together, politically speaking. We're more likely to swipe right on someone who shares our political leanings. And couples with differing political views? They tend to report lower relationship satisfaction and higher conflict. It's like trying to mix oil and water, or, you know, a Democrat and a Republican at Thanksgiving dinner.

But here's the thing: love is messy. It doesn't always follow neat little research studies. Sometimes, opposites do attract. And sometimes, those opposites have very different opinions about, well, everything.

Take another couple: Maria, a free-spirited artist, and David, a buttoned-down accountant. They couldn't be more different politically. Maria marches for climate action, while David quietly supports policies that prioritize economic growth. Yet, they adore each other. Their secret? They've learned to navigate their differences with respect and humor. They avoid hot-button topics at the dinner table and focus on the values they do share: a love for their family, a passion for their hobbies, and a deep commitment to making their community a better place.

So, what's the key to making it work when you're politically mismatched? It's not about changing each other's minds (good luck with that!). It's about understanding each other's perspectives, even if you don't agree with them. It's about finding common ground, focusing on shared values, and learning to laugh at yourselves (and maybe each other's political rants).

And let's not forget the digital elephant in the room. Social media has amplified political polarization, creating echo chambers where we're constantly bombarded with opinions that reinforce our own. It's easy to get caught up in the online fray, firing off angry tweets and demonizing anyone who disagrees with us. But if we want to build bridges instead of walls, we need to step back from the keyboard and engage in real, face-to-face conversations.

The truth is, navigating political differences in a relationship is a challenge. But it's also an opportunity for growth, empathy, and deeper understanding. In a world that's increasingly divided, learning to love across the political aisle might just be the most radical – and most rewarding – thing we can do.

The Ripple Effect: When Politics Crashes the Dinner Party of Love

Let's be honest, folks. "The personal is political" isn't just a catchy slogan anymore; it's the soundtrack to our lives. We used to think we could neatly separate our private lives from the noisy world of politics, but that's like trying to keep oil and water from mixing – a messy, futile endeavor. These days, social movements, political upheavals, and the daily news cycle seep into our homes, our conversations, and yes, even our relationships. It's like that one loud, opinionated uncle at Thanksgiving dinner – you can't ignore it, and it's bound to ruffle some feathers.

Think about it. Remember when discussions about family planning or healthcare were considered private? Now they're prime-time political fodder. This politicization of everything inevitably spills into our relationships. Our values, shaped by our upbringing and experiences, influence who we're attracted to, how we communicate, and what we expect from a partner. When social and political issues become a battleground, those underlying differences, which might have simmered quietly before, can erupt like a volcano.

Social movements, those powerful waves of change, can be both a blessing and a curse for relationships. They're like relationship X-rays, revealing the true strength (or fragility) of the bond.

Shared Values: The Glue That Binds

When couples are on the same page about the big issues – whether it's climate change, racial justice, or LGBTQ+ rights – their shared activism can be incredibly bonding. Imagine two people marching side-by-side for a cause they both believe in. That shared passion, that feeling of fighting for something bigger than themselves, can ignite a deeper connection. It's like having a teammate in the game of life.

Divergent Views: The Wedge That Divides

But what happens when couples find themselves on opposite sides of the fence? Disagreements about fundamental rights and social justice can create a chasm between two people. It's like trying to build a house on a cracked foundation. Suddenly, those dinner table conversations become minefields, each word carefully chosen, each opinion a potential trigger. It's not just about disagreeing; it's about feeling like you don't see eye-to-eye on core values, which can erode respect and trust.

The #MeToo movement, for example, was a watershed moment that exposed the fault lines in many relationships. Some couples found themselves having honest, albeit difficult, conversations about consent and power dynamics, leading to a deeper understanding. For others, it revealed irreconcilable differences, with one partner perhaps a staunch supporter and the other dismissive or skeptical. It was a painful but necessary reckoning.

Then there are political events, like elections, which can feel like a relationship stress test. The current climate of political polarization makes it harder than ever for people with different views to find common ground. It's like everyone's living in their own little echo chamber, only hearing voices that reinforce their existing beliefs. This can lead to couples avoiding political discussions altogether, or worse, engaging in shouting matches that leave everyone feeling hurt and misunderstood.

The 2020 US presidential election was a prime example. Families were torn apart, friendships were fractured, and relationships crumbled under the weight of political disagreement. It wasn't just about voting for different candidates; it was about fundamentally different worldviews clashing.

And let's not forget about current affairs – the curveballs life throws our way. From economic downturns to global pandemics, these events can put immense pressure on relationships.

Shared Stressors: United We Stand

Shared challenges can actually bring couples closer. Navigating a crisis together – whether it's job loss or a health scare – can forge a powerful bond. It's like weathering a storm together and realizing you have a damn good co-captain.

Divergent Coping: When the Road Gets Rocky

But when couples have different ways of coping with stress, things can get tricky. One partner might need to talk things out, while the other might retreat into their shell. One might be anxious, the other calm. These differences can create friction and make it hard to offer support.

The COVID-19 pandemic threw a wrench into everyone's plans, and relationships were no exception. Suddenly, couples were forced to spend 24/7 together, juggling work, childcare, and the constant fear of the unknown. Some couples thrived, rediscovering their connection amidst the chaos. Others struggled, the added stress exacerbating existing tensions. It was a crash course in communication, flexibility, and empathy.

So, how do we navigate this politically charged landscape of love? It's not easy, but it's possible. Open communication is key. Couples need to be able to talk about their differences without resorting to personal attacks. Mutual respect is essential. Even if you disagree with someone's political views, you can still respect them as a person.

It's also important to remember that political beliefs don't define a person entirely. We're all complex individuals with a multitude of facets. Finding common ground on shared values, even amidst political disagreement, can be the key to a strong and resilient relationship. It's about prioritizing the relationship over the political point, listening more than you speak, and understanding that love and respect can, and should, transcend political divides. The personal is political, but it doesn't have to be divisive. With intention and effort, couples can navigate the political landscape of their relationships and emerge stronger, wiser, and maybe even a little more tolerant.

Parenting Partnerships: Raising the Next Generation Together

Sharing the Joy: Rethinking Parenthood in the 21st Century

Forget the image of mom in the kitchen and dad at the office. Parenting in today's world is evolving, and a big part of that evolution is the rise of shared parenting. It's not just about splitting custody; it's a fundamental shift in how we understand motherhood and fatherhood, moving away from rigid, outdated roles and embracing a more balanced, collaborative approach.

Think of it as a partnership. Imagine a dance where both parents are equally graceful, leading and following in turns, always attuned to the music of their children's needs. Shared parenting is about both parents actively participating in the messy, beautiful, and sometimes chaotic reality of raising kids. It's about sharing the midnight feedings, the school plays, the doctor's appointments, and everything in between.

This means more than just dividing tasks. It's about truly sharing the responsibility. It's about both parents being fully invested in their children's lives, from the mundane to the monumental. It's about making decisions together, from choosing a preschool to navigating tricky teenage years. It's about both parents being emotionally available, offering love, support, and guidance every step of the way.

And let's be honest, it's about time! Traditional gender roles have held us back for far too long. They've boxed parents into narrow definitions of what it means to be a mother or a father, limiting both parents and children. Shared parenting breaks down those walls, freeing parents to embrace the full spectrum of parenthood. Mothers can pursue their careers and passions without feeling guilty, while fathers can experience the deep joy of hands-on parenting, building stronger bonds with their children.

But this shift isn't just good for parents; it's fantastic for kids! Research consistently shows that children thrive when they have active, loving relationships with both parents. They tend to have higher self-esteem, do better in school, and have fewer behavioral problems. Why? Because they have two pillars of support, two sources of love and guidance, helping them navigate the world.

Now, let's be real, shared parenting isn't always a walk in the park. It requires open communication, a willingness to compromise, and a shared commitment to putting the children first. There will be disagreements, differing opinions, and moments when you want to pull your hair out. But that's parenting in general, right? The key is to approach these challenges as a team, focusing on what's best for your kids.

Think of it like this: you're building a house together. You might have different ideas about the paint color or the landscaping, but you're both working towards the same goal: creating a warm, loving home for your family. Shared parenting is about building that house together, brick by brick, with love, respect, and a whole lot of teamwork.

So, let's raise a glass (of milk, of course!) to shared parenting. It's a bold step towards a more equitable and fulfilling future for families, a future where both parents are empowered to share the joys and challenges of raising the next generation. It's a future where children have the love and support of both parents, helping them grow into happy, healthy, and well-adjusted adults. And isn't that what we all want?

17.3: Growing Up in Warp Speed: Raising Kids in a World on the Move

Imagine trying to build a sandcastle during a hurricane. That's kind of what parenting feels like these days. The world is spinning faster than ever, a whirlwind of tech, shifting social landscapes, and a beautiful, messy explosion of cultures. How do we, as parents, not just keep our kids upright but actually help them thrive in this dynamic, ever-changing world? It's a big question, and honestly, there's no single right answer. But let's explore some of the key areas shaping childhood today, the challenges and the incredible opportunities they present.

Digital Natives in a Digital World: The Double-Edged Scroll

Our kids are digital natives. They've never known a world without smartphones, the internet, or endless cat videos. Technology is woven into the fabric of their lives, offering incredible educational resources, connecting them with friends across the globe, and giving them platforms for creative expression we could only dream of. But let's be real, it's also a bit of a wild west out there.

Brain in Beta Mode: Think of a young brain like a new computer, constantly being updated. Too much screen time can overload the system, hindering language development, focus, and even empathy. It's like trying to run too many programs at once – things start to lag. Remember that study in the Journal of the American Academy of Pediatrics? They found a real link between screen time in toddlers and later attention problems. It's not about demonizing technology, but about finding a healthy balance.

The Social Media Mirror: Social media can be a tricky space, especially for teens navigating the already-turbulent waters of adolescence. The curated, often unrealistic portrayals of life can lead to feelings of inadequacy and comparison. It's easy to fall into the trap of thinking everyone else is having a better time. Cyberbullying, online harassment, and the pressure to project a perfect online image can take a serious toll on mental health. A 2024 report by the Cyberbullying Research Center highlighted a disturbing rise in anxiety and depression linked to online harassment. We need to equip our kids with the tools to navigate these spaces safely and responsibly.

Navigating the Digital Tightrope: So, what can we do? First, set boundaries. Think "phone-free zones" (dinner table, anyone?) and reasonable screen time limits. Talk to your kids about online safety, responsible digital citizenship, and the potential pitfalls of social media. And, perhaps most importantly, model healthy tech habits ourselves. Put down your phone and engage with your kids in the real world.

Digital Superpowers: But let's not forget the amazing things technology can do. Educational apps can make learning fun, coding websites can unlock a child's inner programmer, and online communities can connect kids with others who share their passions. It's about guiding them to use technology as a tool for growth, not just a distraction.

Beyond Pink and Blue: Expanding the Gender Spectrum

The old idea of gender as a simple binary (boy/girl) is fading, and about time. We're realizing that gender identity is a spectrum, a beautiful and complex tapestry of experiences. There's a growing understanding and acceptance of transgender, non-binary, and genderfluid identities. This shift has huge implications for how we raise our children and create truly inclusive environments.

What's in a Name (and Pronoun)? Gender identity is that deep, internal sense of who you are – male, female, both, neither, or somewhere else entirely. It's different from biological sex, which is assigned at birth. And it's also different from gender expression, which is how someone outwardly presents their gender. A person's gender identity may or may not align with their assigned sex or their gender expression. Kids start developing a sense of their gender identity from a very young age.

Creating a Safe Harbor: For kids exploring their gender identity, support is everything. Listen to them, respect their chosen name and pronouns, and connect them with resources and support networks like LGBTQ+ organizations. Let them know they are loved and accepted for who they are.

Shattering Stereotypes: We can all play a part in breaking down outdated gender stereotypes. Encourage your kids to explore a wide range of interests, regardless of what society tells them is "appropriate" for their gender. Let your daughter build robots and your son explore painting. The possibilities are endless.

Building Inclusive Communities: Schools and communities need to step up too. This means implementing policies that protect transgender and gender non-conforming students from discrimination, providing gender-neutral facilities, and educating everyone about gender diversity. A recent case in California, where a school district implemented a policy allowing students to use the restroom that aligns with their gender identity, shows how things are shifting legally and socially.

A World of Wonders: Embracing Cultural Diversity

Our world is a global village. Raising kids who are culturally competent and celebrate differences isn't just a nice thing to do; it's essential for building a more just and harmonious future.

Bridging Cultures: Cultural competence is about more than just knowing facts about different cultures. It's about understanding our own biases, learning about others with open hearts and minds, and developing the communication skills to bridge cultural gaps.

Planting Seeds of Inclusivity: Expose your kids to the richness of different cultures through books, music, food, and, most importantly, interactions with people from diverse backgrounds. Learning a second language is a fantastic way to open their minds to new perspectives. Attend cultural festivals, visit museums, and make friends from different walks of life.

Confronting Prejudice: Don't shy away from conversations about prejudice and discrimination. Use current events as teachable moments to discuss issues of social justice and equality. Teach your children the importance of treating everyone with respect, regardless of their race, ethnicity, religion, or any other difference.

Education as a Catalyst: Schools have a vital role to play in fostering cultural understanding. Curricula should reflect the diversity of the student body, and schools should create opportunities for students to interact with people from different backgrounds. Multicultural days, cultural exchange programs, and community outreach projects can make a real difference.

The Adventure Continues:

Parenting in the 21st century is an adventure, a journey of constant learning and growth. There's no map, and the terrain is always shifting. But by embracing the challenges and opportunities presented by technology, evolving gender identities, and increasing cultural diversity, we can equip our kids with the skills and values they need to thrive. It's about fostering critical thinking, nurturing empathy, and creating safe, inclusive spaces where every child feels valued and respected. And remember, we're all in this together. Let's support each other, learn from each other, and create a better world for the next generation.

About Author

Dr. Azhar ul Haque Sario is a bestselling author and data scientist with a remarkable record of achievement. This Cambridge alumnus brings a wealth of knowledge to his work, holding an MBA, ACCA (Knowledge Level - FTMS College Malaysia), BBA, and several Google certifications, including specializations in Google Data Analytics, Google Digital Marketing & E-commerce, and Google Project Management.

With ten years of business experience, Azhar combines practical expertise with his impressive academic background to craft insightful books. His prolific writing has resulted in an astounding 2810 published titles, earning him the record for the maximum Kindle editions and paperback books published by an individual author in one year, awarded by Asia Books of Records in 2024. This extraordinary achievement has also led to Azhar being awarded an honorary PhD from World Records University UK, which he will soon receive.

ORCID: https://orcid.org/0009-0004-8629-830X
Azhar.sario@hotmail.co.uk
https://www.linkedin.com/in/azharulhaquesario/

www.ingramcontent.com/pod-product-compliance
Ingram Content Group UK Ltd.
Pitfield, Milton Keynes, MK11 3LW, UK
UKHW040752060225
454761UK00004B/290